MOVING FAITH INTO ACTION

A FACILITATOR'S GUIDE FOR CREATING PARISH SOCIAL MINISTRY ORGANIZATIONS

BY

James R. Lund
and Mary L. Heidkamp

Paulist Press
New York/Mahwah

Interior art by Stella DeVenuta

Book design by Nighthawk Design.

Copyright © 1990 by James R. Lund and Mary L. Heidkamp

Library of Congress Cataloging-in-Publication Data

Lund, James R.
    Moving faith into action: a facilitator's guide for creating parish social ministry organizations/by James R. Lund and Mary L. Heidkamp.
      p. cm.
    Includes bibliographical references.
    ISBN 0-8091-3157-9
    1. Church work—Catholic Church—Societies, etc. 2. Sociology, Christian (Catholic)—Study and teaching (Continuing education)—United States. 3. Christianity and justice—United States—Societies, etc. 4. Catholic Church—United States—Adult education—Societies, etc. 5. Church and social problems—United States—Societies, etc. 6. Church and social problems—Catholic Church—Societies, etc. I. Heidkamp, Mary L. II. Title.
BX2347.2.L85   1990
259—dc20
                                                 90-30842
                                                 CIP

Published by Paulist Press
997 Macarthur Boulevard
Mahwah, New Jersey 07430

Printed and bound in the
United States of America

Contents

*To Bob and Virginia Lund
and Herb (1922–1985) and Mary Anne Heidkamp
Loving Parents who taught us to care
and to Maura and Matthew
Children who keep us caring*

Preface

Moving Faith Into Action has been in process virtually as long as we have known each other. In October, 1977, we met when we began working for the Community Affairs Office of the Diocese of Providence. It was our task to increase awareness of the church's social mission in the parishes of the diocese and to develop leaders in those parishes to carry out that mission.

For two years we spent a great deal of time listening. We listened to people in parishes articulate what they needed and express what they wanted us (the diocesan social action office) to do to assist them. It became very clear that people wanted training that could help them to be effective. Over and over people voiced a hunger for more knowledge of theology and church social teaching. They also raised the question of the need for group dynamic and social action skills, and a desire to integrate all of this with prayer.

In addition, we benefited from exposure to a variety of Catholic social action leaders affiliated with the Catholic Committee on Urban Ministry (CCUM). Harry Fagan, Marge Tuite, David O'Brien, and John Coleman were among the CCUM people who influenced us at that time.

The result of all this probing and listening was the development and piloting of our first multiple-session training process that integrated the four basic elements that comprise the core of the process explained in this book: theology, group process skills, social action skills, and spirituality.

The process has undergone numerous revisions during the intervening years. It has gradually evolved to its present shape after working with it in the Diocese of Rochester, where Mary served as Director of the Department of Justice and Peace and Jim worked as Social Ministry Education Coordinator from 1980 through 1986, and after further refinement in the Archdiocese of Louisville, where Jim directed the Archdiocesan Peace and Justice Center and Mary offered consultant services to dioceses, church agencies and parishes.

Many people in these various places have had a hand in the development of *Moving Faith Into Action.* Maria LoBiondo, who worked with us in shaping the process in Providence, was instrumental in getting it off the ground. Rochester contributors included: Jim Hart, Dominic Aquila, Anne Wegman, Rev. Charlie Mulligan, Joe Torma, Anna Martin, Melissa Marquez and Lourdes Perez-Albuerne. The Louisville Peace and Justice Center staff—Elizabeth Betz, Eileen Blanton, Cherie Cova, Julie Driscoll and Marcy Mossholder—have provided great encouragement and support to help the book to its completion.

We also wish to acknowledge Bishop Matthew H. Clark of Rochester, and Archbishop Thomas C. Kelly, O.P. of Louisville for their staunch support in implementing the church's social mission in their respective dioceses.

Special thanks go to Harry Fagan, whose book, *Empowerment,* is the source of many of the ideas on social action included in this process, and whose friendship and mentoring through the years has guided us in fascinating careers in church-based social action.

Foreword

To be honest, I usually don't read forewords because they mostly seem to be written to get me to buy and read a book that I've bought and already started to read or I would never have seen the foreword in the first place. And I suspect that some forewords are written to promote or put a particular slant on an idea that hasn't been dealt with in the pages that follow. So let me quickly say that my intent here is to do neither. If anything, I want to congratulate you for finding and buying *Moving Faith Into Action,* and urge you to try to do it. Kind of a pat on the back with a little extra nudge—like the Irish compliment of "you look good, have you been sick?" For I am positively delighted that you've wound up with this book in your hands and I assume you plan to use it in your parish. At least I hope so.

After some twenty years of attending social justice meetings in church basements all over the country, I think I have finally developed a rather simple equation.

People are good and want to be empowered to act, when they *believe* it is a matter of acting out their faith, when they *understand* the facts of the situation, when they have an *attitude* that helps them to identify with those who are suffering or being put upon in some way, and when they have a chance to develop a few *skills* that will give them enough confidence to try to do something.

Having met Jim's and Mary's fresh young faces at Notre Dame in a CCUM workshop about fifteen years ago, and after working with and watching them grow in wisdom and commitment through their social action jobs in the diocese of Providence, then Rochester, then Louisville and now Chicago, I think it is wonderful that they have been able to bring together all their church basement learnings about how to help people focus on their belief, understanding, attitudinal and skill needs in this easy-to-read facilitator's guide for creating parish social ministry organizations. What a gift these two are and have given to the church and its social mission!

In some respects, this gift is simply a social justice adult education process that works. Works because it moves people to act. God knows we need this kind of a proven tool in all our parishes, not only because the folks have a right to know what their responsibilities are in relation to all the what's and why's of the church's social teachings from a hundred years ago or even yesterday. More importantly, without people's support and participation in this tradition we can't expect anything to change. Also, and not incidentally, one of the things I like most about Jim's and Mary's adult education process is that it actually treats people like adults—an all too rare happening these days.

I have long thought that a good parish social action leader needs a strong discipline of specificity, a solid grounding in faith, a wonderful sense of humor, and, above all, a goal directed toward the development of people as a crucial key to any solution-oriented social action. After reading this extremely usable (almost paint by the numbers) manual, I'm sure you'll agree with me that Jim's and Mary's warmth and high energy jump from the pages and blend well with their basic optimism about the world and positive approach to underscoring the need for discipline in our church's activism.

Harry Fagan
Managing Director
National Pastoral Life Center

Introduction

Roman Catholic involvement in social issues has grabbed the headlines of our nation's newspapers and the lead stories of network news programs on a number of occasions in recent years. The U.S. bishops' recent pastoral letters, the 1983 *Challenge of Peace* and the 1986 *Economic Justice for All,* drew widespread public attention, not only when they were approved, but during their drafting process as well. Pope John Paul II generates much media attention whenever he speaks, and he speaks often about issues of importance to Catholics in the United States, issues such as the arms race, abortion, and economic injustice. Such a high profile among Catholic leaders means, among other things, that the church has been taking seriously its mission to act on behalf of justice and to work for peace.

Few make the mistake, however, of concluding that by the hierarchy's gaining headlines the work is done. On the contrary, the social mission's greatest challenge lies before the church. At the end of "Justice in the World," the Second Synod of Bishops declared, "The examination of conscience which we have made together, regarding the church's involvement in action for justice, will remain ineffective if it is not given flesh in the life of our local churches at all their levels."[1] Similar sentiments closed the American hierarchy's recent pastoral letters, as they stated in the final chapters of each, that these pastoral letters represented the beginning, not the end, of long-term efforts.

Whatever these efforts might entail, moving the church's mission to work for justice and peace into the center of parish life must be counted as one of the most important steps. How to do that continues to be one of the most frequently asked questions by diocesan social action directors, parish staff persons, and others who hope to see the U.S. Catholic Church mature in this direction.

1. Second Synod of Bishops, *Justice in the World,* 1971, para. 72.

The answers to it are understandably many and necessarily incomplete.

This book represents one such response. With no claim to be *the* answer, it does provide one answer to the troubling question of how to move parishes into social action.

Specifically, it details a process that has been used in parishes in various dioceses around the country. It provides a would-be facilitator with just about all the background needed to get a parish social ministry committee off and running. We have used the process successfully in the three dioceses where we have worked. Perhaps more importantly, an early draft of this book has been used as the basic resource to get committees started in dioceses where we have never been. The Diocese of Grand Rapids, for example, used this process in their successful follow-up to Season III of RENEW. It served parishes there as they put into practice the deeper understanding of the church's social mission which RENEW engendered.

We think that it works because it resulted from prolonged and careful listening to experts in theology, social action, spirituality and, most especially, experts from parishes: staff members and lay people who helped us understand their needs and who critiqued our efforts to respond to them.

In the decade during which we have worked with Catholic parishes, certain knowledge and skills have consistently shown themselves to be needed for any group that sought successfully to engage in church-based social action. First, the groups require a fundamental understanding of the theological basis of the church's mission to work for justice and peace. Next, they need working skills in group process, skills that any successful group must have. Also, a particular need for a social ministry group is the familiarity with social action skills. One of the most daunting challenges a committee faces is focusing on a social problem and generating an effective response to it. These skills help do this. Finally, a church social action group must ground itself in a spirituality that recognizes that following Jesus Christ demands taking, not escaping from, responsibility to transform the world.

These four knowledge and skill areas form the backbone of the Parish Social Ministry Organizing Process explained in this book. What makes it somewhat unique is that they all appear in the same place, and they are woven together in a fashion that evokes a synergistic result. What makes them work effectively is the methodology used.

The process design incorporates basic principles of adult education. It presumes that participants are self-directed, and it fosters the development of increased self-direction. It acknowledges the value of the experience of each person, and draws on that experience as a resource to the process itself. It endeavors to enhance social skills that can be applied immediately, and in a wide variety of contexts. Finally, it is fully participatory. The group controls the essential outcome of the process, which itself only facilitates the formation of a vibrant parish social ministry organization.

When we started doing this work, we found these different pieces in different places. The theologians could speak and write about the church's social mission, but if they knew how to put it into action, they weren't telling. Social action folks could organize well enough, but didn't usually draw on one of the most potent motivators of church people: prayer. In short, it seemed no one had put it together in a way that applied easily to the reality of a typical parish.

This process arose to meet that need, and to enable parish groups to make social ministry come alive in their local communities. Both its content and its methodology demonstrate a sensitivity to the people who take part in the process. Consequently, it has served as an effective instrument in a variety of parishes to bring social ministry to life in the heart of the parish.

Overview of Manual

This facilitator's manual contains detailed descriptions for group leaders to use in each of the six organizing sessions that comprise this process. In each session, the facilitator is provided with the following:

- A brief introduction explaining the elements of the session and the rationale for them.
- An agenda with time specifications.
- A listing of session objectives and description of what must be done to prepare for the session.
- Detailed notes for each agenda item.
- Briefing papers offering detailed notes for lectures.
- Handouts to be copied and distributed to each participant.

To use the process, participants will need two additional resources: copies of *Justice in the World* and *This Land is Home to Me. Justice in the World* is available in two formats. The United States Catholic Conference Office of Printing and Publication Services has copies of the document in its original form. The Campaign for Human Development (CHD) has published *To Campaign for Justice,* a booklet that contains the original document and a paraphrased version which appeals to people who may be uncomfortable with theological language. *This Land is Home to Me* is available from the Catholic Committee of Appalachia (Whitesburg, KY 41858).

The only audio-visual production suggested for use is the videotape entitled, "Building Partnerships." The Campaign For Human Development produced it in 1988, and provided a copy to every diocesan CHD director. This is likely to be available from diocesan social action offices, but if it isn't, it can be purchased from CHD for $5.95.

OVERVIEW OF THE ORGANIZING PROCESS

Four Key Content Areas

Theology

A group's understanding of and consensus on its mission is the basic ingredient of a successful organization. Without it the best group process skills will fail to have an effect. With it other shortcomings can be overcome. The theology that grounds social concern in Christian faith provides a necessary foundation for a parish social ministry group's mission.

This process utilizes several sources in conveying some of the major features of this theology. A survey overview of Catholic Social Teaching occurs in Session I, and is followed in Session III with a consideration of the Second Synod of Bishops' 1971 statement, *Justice in the World.* The fourth session continues the treatment of the social teaching through the study of *This Land is Home to Me,* a pastoral letter which the Catholic bishops of Appalachia issued in 1975 and reaffirmed in 1985.

The scriptural bases for social concern serve as the focus of reflection and discussion in Session II. This often provides the most meaningful hour of the entire process. Group after group become absorbed in the discussion of holy scripture, and are genuinely moved by the profoundly social implications found in the passages studied. This step provides a solid foundation for the subsequent study of social teaching. Through both scripture and social teaching the central place which social concern occupies in the Roman Catholic tradition becomes apparent to participants.

Recent U.S. bishops' statements have indeed rectified some of the ignorance among Catholics that has surrounded both our social teaching and the social implications of the Bible. The surprised reaction of many to *The Challenge of Peace,* and *Economic Justice for All* showed precisely how unfamiliar many were with this aspect of our faith. Reading some of the more provocative biblical passages and some documents from the corpus of Catholic social teaching similarly surprises some who take part in this process. One man stood up in a session several years ago and said, "Why has it taken over ten years for me, an active, church-going Catholic, to hear about *Justice in the World?*" Such reactions will continue to be the case, although the pastoral letters may have cut down the number. They have not, however, erased the need for the accent that processes such as this place on theology, and so, scripture and social teaching need to be a cornerstone of any process designed to enable church-based social ministry.

Group Process Skills

Group skills serve as the second content area found in this process. While the transformation of American Catholicism to a full-fledged voluntary association may not yet be complete, voluntarism fully characterizes participation in groups such as parish social ministry organizations. For a group to thrive in such a context, effective use of group process skills is necessary.

A number of these skills are worked on over the course of the six-session process. The topic of leadership is handled in several ways as discussions focus on both its nature and its tasks. The roles that have to be carried out in a successful group are explored, as are the topics of conflict resolution and meeting preparation. Useful techniques such as brainstorming and skills such as prioritizing are both introduced and exercised.

The group skills covered represent a variety of the ones most useful to a volunteer group. Even when some members may have more experience in group leadership than others, the common foundation serves to facilitate the whole group's inner workings. A side benefit of this skill development comes from its attractiveness to participants. People find that they can transfer the skills practiced in the program to a variety of other life situations, ranging from other volunteer involvements to business or work responsibilities.

Social Action Skills

Social action skills may not have the same broad applicability as these others, but they are essential for parish social ministry organizations. A frequently paralyzing dilemma for these groups is posed by the infinite possibilities for involvement. The media raises at least one major, compelling social issue a week that could occupy the full attention of thousands of parish groups. Every community and neighborhood has shortcomings that positive social action could address, and global issues always intrude into the consciousness of caring people and groups. The skills covered in this process help the group to focus and to choose priority concerns.

Specifically, participants identify problems they could address, prioritize them according to a suggested set of criteria, and devise appropriate responses. The facilitator guides each of these steps, careful to enable the group to set its own action agenda, and determine its own strategies.

Engaging in actions which have measurable results should be one of the primary intentions of any social action organization. This area of the organizing process provides the framework for realizing this intention.

Spirituality

When we first began working in the church social action business, a caricature of church activists depicted us as people who were constantly doing, but never praying. To whatever extent that reflected the reality ten years ago, we would say it no longer has any validity. The social concerns of the church are rooted in the spiritual lives of her people, and the social action of the church draws from this well.

The prayer and spirituality in this process reflects the integrated model which the U.S. bishops promote in the closing section of *The Challenge of Peace.* The pastoral says, "A conversion of our hearts and minds will make it possible for us to enter into a closer communion with our Lord. We nourish that communion by personal and communal prayer, for it is in prayer that we encounter Jesus, who is our peace, and learn from him the way to peace."[1] Prayer thus serves as the wellspring for the Christian life that exhibits love of God and love of neighbor.

The spirituality encouraged in this process is built around prayer themes that would deepen one's sense of social responsibility. Each session's prayer focuses on topics like compassion, discipleship, the option for the poor, and the reign of God. In this way the process emphasizes the importance of prayer's integration with action.

Variations on the Content

The elements of this process have been carefully chosen and have been frequently tested. Nothing that didn't work remains, and nothing that has been untried is included. At the same time, considerable room for adaptation exists.

The choice of church teachings and the prayer services used in the process are just two of the content areas that could easily be adapted for groups for which other choices might be more appropriate. For example, the 1979 pastoral letter *Brothers and Sisters to Us* could substitute for *This Land is Home to Me* in Session IV, if that pastoral's treatment of racism would be a better subject for discussion than "This Land's" poetic consideration of powerlessness in Appalachia. The prayer services, meanwhile, are limited only by our own preferences. We believe the themes present points of reflection germane to social ministry, but know well that there are many ways of raising them in prayer. In these two areas, especially, adaptation is encouraged.

Format and Methodology

The process usually takes place in the context of six two-and-a-half-hour sessions, spaced with a week between them.

1. National Conference of Catholic Bishops, *The Challenge of Peace*, 1983, para. 290.

As important as the content is, an equally significant concern is the manner in which it is conveyed. In this process, as much care is given, therefore, to method as to content.

In constructing this Parish Social Ministry Organizing Process a number of factors weighed heavily in determining its shape. First, since the process is one of adult education, principles pertaining to adult learning have been utilized. Second, realizing that a two-and-a-half-hour evening program must move quickly to keep people interested, each session includes a variety of different activities, and no time is wasted. Third, given the goal of formation or rejuvenation of a working organization, each session builds upon the others with the first session presuming little, and the last session assuming the group is ready to carry out its agenda. The result is a varied, interesting process that, in our experience, ninety percent of the original participants complete.

Fifteen hours represents a significant commitment on the part of the parish people who sign up for this process. It is not, however, a great deal of time to accomplish the objectives of the process. Accordingly, participants also are requested to do preparation for each session. This involves reading, some reflection, and a bit of research. As with the process itself, the preparation requests are judiciously chosen and really represent the minimum needed for the process to work.

Session I breaks open the four content areas of the process while also facilitating the ice-breaking needed at the outset. It uses group process activities to introduce participants to subjects like social ministry, and leadership skills. A pre-test in Catholic social teaching provides a provocative beginning to the consideration of theology, and a prayer service focused on compassion roots the group in a spiritual quality essential for social ministers.

The next session handles two major subjects. The first is the scriptural basis for social concern. The second pertains to group process skills.

Session III continues the treatment of theology with a close look at *Justice in the World*. It also deals with conflict resolution and leadership qualities. Finally, the groundwork is being laid for the identification and prioritization of problems that the organization will consider.

In Session IV, theology continues with study of *This Land is Home to Me,* and the link between faith and social action is made through a look at projects funded by the Campaign for Human Development. Participants also identify the problems they want the organization to address.

Session V focuses exclusively on selecting priorities. Session VI wraps up the process with final words on spirituality, theology and group process. Also, Session VI includes task force meetings at which task forces work on defining the actions they will take to address the problems they have chosen.

Accompanying each session are a series of handouts which are used in the process. They are used both for activities and for conveying information. Some, like the handouts on conflict resolution, are quite detailed. The handouts facilitate participation, and some provide useful resources for future reference.

Overall, the key to the process is participation of the group. In all areas it is encouraged and modeled. The success of the organizing process depends upon the people in the organization taking full responsibility for it. The method, format and content all unite to make that happen.

Setting Up the Organizing Process

The quality of the preparation for the Organizing Process will, in large measure, determine how successful the process will be. Getting a parish social ministry organization started or revived requires a fairly substantial commitment on the part of everyone involved. Most directly, this refers to the parish staff, the parish's lay leadership, and the people who will participate in the process and organization. Good preparation will convincingly invite these people to support the effort.

A second key task is securing the services of a competent facilitator. While it is possible for someone connected with the parish to serve in this capacity, most frequently the facilitator comes from outside the parish. In any event, lining up facilitators is another key preparatory task.

As a parish moves toward this process, it is instructive to envision the stages through which it passes. Preparation can thus be more complete, and the tasks clearly identified. The stages look like this:

	Preliminary: Decision is made to organize.
	Facilitators enlisted. Promotion plan developed.
Weeks 1–4	Promotion: Four–five week period of lining up participants.
Week 5	Informational meeting to describe process to interested parishioners.
Weeks 6–12	Process: Six-session process.
Week 13 or 14	Follow-up: Short-term includes parish commissioning ceremony.

The timespan for this covers about three months.

PROMOTING THE PROCESS

The Social Ministry Organizing Process responds, we believe, to a distinct and important need. Like other needs, the value of a parish social ministry organization is not always apparent to some key people. Consequently, the initiator of the process has to sell it to the key actors in a particular parish.

For church folk, talk of selling may seem inappropriate. It is a useful concept, however, to consider here with regard to motivating parish staff people and members to commit themselves.

Given the fact that we have developed and written this book, we find it very easy to sell. Testimonies that people have made over the years extolling the process have led us to believe very deeply that it does deliver on its promise to facilitate the organization of parish social ministry groups. One pastoral associate, who had been disappointed by other attempts to organize such efforts and who consequently looked upon this process with skepticism, embraced us after the six sessions and said, "You were right. It did work!" The retailer of the process, therefore, must believe in the product and help others believe in it.

Whether or not this individual is working, as we have, from a diocesan base, or is coming at the organizing process from within the parish, the keys to its success are the same. The first two keys relate to selling the process. In order for this to work, parish staff support and ample participation of parish members must be assured. The third key pertains to finding people to facilitate the process.

Parish Staff Support

For anyone remotely familiar with the power structure of a typical American parish, it is clear that a necessary early step in planning any parish activity is gaining the assent and support of the parish staff. Further, for something like this Social Ministry Organizing Process to fly, the staff's commitment to the process and its purpose must be resolute.

In seeking such a commitment, a specific delineation of the things being asked of the staff ought to be provided. The staff role involves promotion of the process, and a commitment to follow up on it. Specifically, we suggest, the following three elements be incorporated into the commitment which the parish staff makes:

- Promote the organizing process and commit to recruiting lay leaders.
- One staff member participate in the organizing process.
- Agree to short and long term follow-up, short-term would involve planning a commissioning of the group and long-term would call for ongoing staffing for the committee.

Gaining this support may require careful strategy. Many parish staffs are stretched thinly over many obligations and responsibilities. This process should be suggested, therefore, not as something that will stretch them even further, but as something that will be able to help them minister more effectively. Fewer and fewer parish staff members in this decade of groundbreaking pastoral letters and papal encyclicals refuse to acknowledge the importance of the church's social mission. This does not mean, however, that they all know how to implement it. This process, if presented to seemingly resistant or disinterested staff as something that can help them, could turn the tide from apathy to enthusiasm. Several years ago, a staff member from the Diocese of Orlando related how a pastor, hostile to the work of the diocesan office, became one of its strongest supporters after this process launched a parish social ministry organization in his parish.

Ample Participation of Parish Members

This process needs between twelve and twenty people to work effectively. Ample, therefore, means between twelve and twenty. Yet, it also has a secondary meaning. Ample also refers to who these participants are, and what they bring to the group.

Promotion of the organizing process is directed toward turning out this ample group. Most obviously, the promotion involves letting the parish know the process is happening, and inviting interested members to take part. Bulletin announcements, posters at church entrances, and other more creative approaches can be employed to let the parish know the process will be happening. A homily which accents the church's social mission and informs the congregation of the organizing is important. While personal contacts will, in the end, probably be the most effective approach to recruitment, broad, general invitations need to be blended with them to insure that all in the parish do receive the invitation to take part and because the general appeal itself educates the parish on the church's social mission.

While the mass-media promotion invites any interested parishioner to join in the organizing process, parish staff and lay leaders should identify and recruit people who they believe have something to offer to this area of parish mission. The parish social ministry organization should aspire to have representation from the diversity of the parish. It may be necessary, therefore, to recruit people to guarantee that various age groups, different ethnic and racial groups, and a balance of men and women all participate. Also, while the organizing process does include leadership skills, it does not provide the depth which can transform someone who never has exercised any leadership at all into a competent committee chairperson. Consequently, people with some leadership experience or potential should be sought out.

Effectively asking people to give fifteen hours over six weeks in a bulletin blurb or during a phone call can be a pretty tough sell. A good alternative to trying that is to borrow a technique used often in other fields—the informational meeting. Gaining commitments from people to come to one hour-and-a-half gathering presents less of an obstacle than getting them to sign on to the full six-week process.

We strongly recommend holding this kind of meeting.

As a six-session process does represent a major time commitment, an informational meeting gives people the chance to take a good look at what the process requires so that they can make a well-informed decision before signing their lives away. It will almost totally eliminate attendance of people who could discover halfway through Session I that this process isn't about hosting coffee hour after the 10 o'clock mass.

The informational session also provides the opportunity to get people excited. During the hour-

and-a-half, the leader enthusiastically lays out the process, the schedule of sessions, and the importance of a parish-based social ministry organization. In short, the leader makes a sales pitch.

To summarize, then, promotion of the process needs to be an intentional part of organizing a parish social ministry group. With some creativity and a little bit of work, it can work what otherwise might seem to be a miracle: new and enthusiastic faces anxious to get involved.

Competent Facilitators

Individuals with certain basic skills and knowledge can take the contents of this manual, and use it to help form a parish social ministry organization. Because there is some variety to the skills and knowledge involved, a team of two or three facilitators will, in most cases, be preferable.

Perhaps the most important characteristic of a competent facilitator will be a working understanding of the adult education process. The facilitators' work literally involves making the organization's formation easier. An adult educator will handle this process accordingly, and be anxious to get out of the group's way when it is ready to fly.

The several content areas of the process—theology, group process, social action and spirituality—require some familiarity. There is, however, substantial information on each in the briefing materials. In addition, the bibliography includes references that can add to one's depth in each area.

In setting up the process, then, there are several key steps. Set in a context that permits the time needed to do the stages of the process well, the obtaining of staff support, the attracting of 12–20 diverse, able participants, and the securing of competent facilitators will help assure the development of an effective parish social ministry organization.

SESSION I

Introduction

The first session's design reveals our conviction that a good initial experience is critical to the success of this organizing process. First impressions are lasting impressions, and in this case it must be a good impression if we want people to commit the next six weeks to it. Accordingly, Session I provides a fast-moving, highly participatory agenda that introduces participants to the key elements underlying successful parish social ministry efforts.

These first two-and-a-half hours introduce process and content patterns that will recur during the six-week process.

In terms of process, it is imperative that people know why they are there and that they feel comfortable being there. To facilitate the former, the brief opening prayer anchors the process in Christian faith, and the course overview explains exactly what the group will accomplish over the six weeks. With regard to helping people feel at home, the "Introduction" calls for an icebreaking exercise, and several of the session's agenda items utilize small-group activities.

The issue of time is also a key process concern in this session. At the outset, two-and-a-half hours seems like a major time commitment. Also, since most parish activities occur at night, this means that ending time will usually be 9:30 or 10:00 pm. The process is designed to handle both of these issues. Session I moves very quickly. No one item is scheduled for more than 30 minutes. Like other sessions, the time scheduled after the break is less than the time before, and the items on the agenda are highly participatory and stimulating. If the leader keeps the session moving by adhering to the schedule, participants will assuredly wonder where the time went. When that happens, much of the resistance to "long" sessions will melt away.

The stimulation which the content of the agenda creates also serves to keep people's minds off the clock. In this first session each of the four subjects that are woven through the process receive treatment. Theology is handled through the test on Catholic social teaching, and in the brief lecture that follows it. Group process skills and social ministry skills are covered through structured exercises and discussions. Finally, the opening and closing prayer introduce the spirituality that permeates the process.

Session I gets the process off and running. It introduces people to the key subject areas, whets their appetites for more, and motivates them to follow through.

SESSION I—SUGGESTED USE OF TIME

10 min.	1.	Registration/Handout
5 min.	2.	Prayer
15 min.	3.	Introductions
10 min.	4.	Agenda/Course Overview
25 min.	5.	Testing the Doctrine
30 min.	6.	Exercise: Leadership Qualities
10 min.	7.	Break
30 min.	8.	Exercise: Looking Ahead
15 min.	9.	Prayer
5 min.	10.	Preparation for Session II

SESSION I—LEADER'S PLAN

Objectives

A. Content

1. Introduce group to church social teaching.
2. Explore the nature of social ministry committee work.
3. Consider the qualities of leaders.
4. Reflect on the nature of compassion.

B. Process

1. Break the ice; make the group feel comfortable.

2. Engage group in decision-making task.
3. Facilitate the group's working and praying together.

Preparation

Before the first session, the leader should be familiar with the facilities that will be used. The seating arrangement should allow each participant to see all others, either a semicircle or U-shaped arrangement. Equipment that will be used during each session should be set up prior to the session so that it will be accessible when needed. Newsprint and easel should be set up at the beginning as they will be used prior to the break. The sign-up sheets and ID badges should be in an accessible location near the entrance of the room.

Equipment needed for the first session:

- newsprint and easel
- equipment needed for prayer service

Materials needed for session:

- pocket folders with first session handouts in place
- sign-up sheet, ID badges, writing implements
- magic markers

PROGRAM FOR SESSION I

1. Registration: 10 min.

Participants will sign up, fill in ID badges, and then be given folders with the packet of materials.

Clipped to the front of the packet will be *Handout 1A* which participants will be asked to begin filling out immediately. It is important to start the session on time, and this assignment will give notice to late-comers that the starting time is indeed the starting time. People will be given ten minutes after the scheduled starting time to complete the handout. Instruction will then be given to those who have not completed it to do so after the session.

Beyond starting on time the purpose of this is to stimulate thinking on the part of participants on the subjects that will occupy the group in the

coming weeks. The leader should note that this form will not be collected, but that it may be interesting for individuals to review their answers after they have completed the course.

2. Prayer: 5 min.

The leader will read the Letter of James 2:14–24, and reflect briefly on the scripture.

The reflection should note the connection between James' teaching and the process upon which the group is embarking; that is, to put faith into action by responding to the social concerns that are present in our neighborhood, our community, and our world.

3. Introductions: 15 min.

As well as simply introducing participants to each other, the intention here is to break the ice, to begin to make people feel comfortable with each other.

One icebreaker that always seems to work well is one in which individuals describe themselves with a superlative. Each person is asked to give their name, and perhaps some other brief biographical information, but secondly, she/he is requested to describe themselves in relation to the rest of the group with a superlative. The people are therefore directed to examine the group carefully, and decide in what way they are superlative to all the others. Individuals may claim to be the youngest, oldest, skinniest, shyest, most artistic, and so on. One other element that adds to the interaction is that the group is free to dispute any claim that is made. If someone, for example, claims to be the youngest member of the group, and another can successfully challenge it, then the individual has to make a new claim.

Many other icebreakers could serve the purpose intended here which is simply to relax the group and to begin to make each person comfortable with the others.

An important factor for facilitators is that if a group is much larger than fifteen people the amount of time allocated for this may be insufficient. Appropriate adjustments would then need to be made.

4. Agenda/Course Overview: 10 min.

The leader reviews with the group the agenda for this session, and the outline for the course (*Handout 1B*). The outline is very broad, but it contains an overview of what will be covered in the six sessions. It can be restated that the purpose of the program, as indicated on the overview, is to assist the group(s) in doing the work of SMC's in their parish(es). The various skills necessary for that work will be addressed in the program.

At this time it should be pointed out to the participants that each session builds on what has preceded it, and therefore attendance at every session is important. It should be stressed that the success of the program depends on the active participation of the group as a whole and as individuals both during the sessions and in completing the assignments. The facilitator emphasizes the key role that the preparations will play in the sessions when they are due.

Allow for questions that people may have, and check for their assent for the process.

5. Testing the Doctrine: 25 min.

Handout 1C is a True-False test on Catholic social teaching. The group will be given a few minutes to mark their answers. When it is apparent that almost everyone is finished, the leader begins to review the answers. *Briefing Paper 1* provides the answer key and notes on the questions and answers.

Asking in a general kind of way for participants' responses is an effective way to review the answers. Taking the questions one at a time in this way, the leader gains some idea of how the group did, and will get an impression of what questions caused the most controversy. The leader should give the opportunity for disagreement to be voiced, but not let it go far. Discussion could go on for hours on the topics of private property, the just war theory and the right to a job, and one of the facilitator's most difficult tasks is to cut off what frequently is a very interesting discussion. Other steps for the leader include:

1. Clarifying the correct answers as well as time allows;

2. Reading the appropriate citations if needed;
3. Reiterating that this exercise is only the beginning of the group's consideration of Catholic social teaching, and that there will be ample opportunity to continue the discussion in subsequent weeks.

The theology section closes with a five-minute presentation on the social mission of the church. *Briefing Paper 1* contains the outline for this talk.

Note: While the time allocated for this is only 25 minutes, more time can be allotted if the first four items on the agenda took less than the forty minutes allocated for them.

BRIEFING PAPER 1: REVIEW OF THE PRE-TEST ON CATHOLIC SOCIAL TEACHING

What follows is the answer key for the pre-test on Catholic social teaching, notes on the nature of the teaching, and an outline for a brief lecture on the material. The answer key identifies the document from which the teaching comes; offers an explanation of how people often respond to a given question; and provides clues for the facilitator's response and a pertinent quotation from the teaching.

In reviewing the pre-test, the facilitator must be mindful of time. This exercise could consume much of the session's two-and-a-half hours, so time limits need to be carefully observed. The leader of this section should not intend to convey all the points noted here. Instead, she or he should use only what is necessary to satisfy the group. Reminding the group that this is only an introduction to social teaching and that during the course of the six weeks there will be ample time to continue the discussion works well to move the group quickly through the debriefing.

ANSWER KEY

1. U.S. Catholic Bishops, *The Challenge of Peace*, 1983, paragraph #333.
False.

In the closing section of the National Conference of Catholic Bishops' pastoral letter, *The Challenge of Peace,* the nation's bishops said,

Peacemaking is not an optional commitment. It is a requirement of our faith. We are called to be peacemakers, not by some movement of the moment, but by our Lord Jesus. The content and context of our peacemaking is set, not by some political agenda or ideological program, but by the teaching of His Church.

2. Pope John XXIII, *Peace on Earth* (*Pacem in Terris*), 1963, paragraph #11.
True.
The economic rights noted in this question are among those which John XXIII listed in *Peace on Earth.* Typically, people don't dispute this answer even though it is one example of the contrast between the rights that the church teaches belong to every person, and the rights that the U.S. Constitution protects.

The assertion that each person has "economic rights" in the 1986 U.S. bishops' pastoral letter, *Economic Justice for All,* has drawn fire from some conservative quarters. While our political tradition strongly affirms civil and political rights, it is ambiguous with respect to these economic rights. To be sure, this is one area where Catholic social teaching conflicts with some principal Western political ideologies.

John XXIII's own assertion of these rights could not be clearer as he declares:

Beginning our discussion of the rights of the human person, we see that every person has the right to life, to bodily integrity, and to the means which are suitable for the proper development of life; these are primarily food, clothing, shelter, rest, medical care and finally the necessary social services. Therefore a human being also has the right to security in cases of sickness, inability to work, widowhood, old age, unemployment, or in any other case in which he is deprived of the means of subsistence through no fault of his own.

3. Pope Paul VI, *On the Development of Peoples,* 1967, paragraph #49.
True.
This answer is seldom contested, but individuals may not agree with the teaching. Paul VI speaks clearly and strongly on this point so the teaching obviously supports the answer.

Questions about the teaching vary. I often ask, "Who of us has superfluous wealth?" As few people will admit to it, the question that follows then is, "Who determines what is superfluous?" Our suggestion is the poor are better qualified to make the determination than the non-poor. Another direction that the discussion can take is whether we are called to give only what is superfluous, or whether we must be open to giving of our substance. The more radical implication of the latter is not denied by the former, and it is safe to admit that Christ does call for this giving of substance.

Pope Paul VI directly supports this answer, writing, "We must repeat once more that the superfluous wealth of rich countries should be placed at the service of poor nations."

4. Vatican II, *The Pastoral Constitution on the Church in the Modern World* (*Gaudium et Spes*), 1965, paragraph 43.
True.
The Second Vatican Council's *Pastoral Constitution on the Church in the Modern World* pleaded for Christians to let their faith shine through in all that they do. This council document states:

This Council exhorts Christians, as citizens of two cities, to strive to discharge their earthly duties conscientiously and in response to the Gospel spirit. They are mistaken who, knowing that we have no abiding city but seek one which is to come, think that they may therefore shirk their earthly responsibilities ... This split between the faith which many profess and their daily lives deserves to be counted among the more serious errors of our age. Long since the prophets of the Old Testament fought vehemently against this scandal and even more so did Jesus Christ Himself in the New Testament threaten it with grave punishments.

5. John Paul II, *On Human Labor* (*Laborem Exercens*), 1981, Section #18.
False.
Like question 3, this refers to the body of economic rights which the church teaches are basic human rights. In his 1981 encyclical, Pope John Paul II insists that government does have the responsibility to take action against unemployment. He says,

[T]he opposite of a just and right situation in this field is unemployment, that is to say the lack of work for those who are capable of it ... The role of the agents included under the title of indirect employer [John Paul II defines the state as an indirect employer.] is to act against unemployment which in all cases is an evil and which, when it reaches a certain level, can become a real social disaster.

Later, the Holy Father adds, "In the final analysis this overall concern weighs on the shoulders of the state."

The U.S. bishops reinforce this position in their 1986 pastoral letter *Economic Justice for All.* They assert, "employment is a basic right" (para. 137), and claim, "the burden of securing full employment falls on all of us." This perspective makes clear that the whole society—the public and private sectors—has the responsibility to work for full employment.

6. U.S. Catholic Bishops, *Economic Justice for All,* 1986, paragraph 38.

True.

This is a fairly direct quotation from the American bishops' 1986 pastoral letter. It states,

Central to the biblical presentation of justice is that the justice of a community is measured by its treatment of the powerless in society, most often described as the widow, the orphan, the poor and the stranger (non-Israelite) in the land.

7. Vatican II, *Pastoral Constitution on the Church in the Modern World,* 1964 Paragraph #69, *On the Development of Peoples,* Paragraph #23, and U.S. Bishops, *Economic Justice for All,* Paragraph #114 and #115.

False.

Perhaps more than any other, the question on private property provokes reactions. The answer is false, and that fact grates on the sensibilities of Americans for whom the right is virtually sacred.

"In all conditions" is the clause that makes the statement false. The church does defend the right of private property, but does not do so absolutely. Instead, the teaching on property embodies a dimension of stewardship that considers the common good generally, and the needs of the poor specifically. So considered, private property is a relative and not absolute right.

The three documents cited here are quite explicit in their treatment of the relativity of the right of private property. The "Pastoral Constitution" traces this teaching to the Fathers and Doctors of the church. It asserts, "the right to have a share of earthly goods sufficient for oneself and one's family belongs to everyone." As a consequence of this, the Pastoral Constitution adds, "If a person is in extreme necessity, he has the right to take from the riches of others what he himself needs."

Paul VI affirms this perspective on property. Quoting St. Ambrose, this encyclical says, "You are not making a gift of your possessions to the poor person. You are handing over to him what is his." Property in this view is given by God to all, and those who are rich have usurped a disproportionate amount of the creation. The encyclical concludes its section on this topic with another concrete embodiment of the Catholic understanding of the principle of private property.

"If certain landed estates impede the general prosperity," Paul VI said, "because they are extensive, unused or poorly used, or because they bring hardship to peoples or are detrimental to the interests of the country, the common good sometimes demands their appropriation." This declaration demonstrates the relativity of the right of private property and its subservience to the common good.

The U.S. bishops develop these same themes when discussing property in *Economic Justice for All.* They use John Paul II's term "social mortgage" to convey the limits that the right to private property implies. They also emphasize the desirability of broad-based ownership of both personal and productive property.

A final note—the leader of this discussion should keep two things in mind. First, "in all conditions," is a key phrase. The church does not morally object to private property per se. But, as the above discussion indicates, its acceptance of it is qualified. Second, this question provokes strong reactions. Therefore, it is important to permit expression of them while calmly presenting the church's position.

8. Vatican II, "Pastoral Constitution," para. 80, and *The Challenge of Peace,* para. 104.

True.

The just war principles which have been a part of Catholic moral theology since St. Augustine hold that any act of war must discriminate between combatants and noncombatants. Counter-population warfare fails in the test of being discriminate. In *The Challenge of Peace,* the U.S. bishops state:

The lives of innocent persons may never be taken directly regardless of the purpose alleged for doing so. To wage truly "total" war is by definition to take huge numbers of innocent lives.

The bishops later quote the Pastoral Constitution on this issue.

Any act of war aimed indiscriminately at the destruction of entire cities or of extensive areas along with their population is a crime against God and humanity. It merits unequivocal and unhesitating condemnation.

9. Pope John Paul II, *The Social Concern of the Church (Sollicitudo Rei Socialis),* 1988, Section 27–31 and *Justice in the World,* paras. 47–48.
    True.
Pope John Paul II startled some readers of his latest encyclical with his clarity on the issue of church possessions. He said,

Faced by cases of need, one cannot ignore them in favor of superfluous church ornaments and costly furnishings for divine worship; on the contrary it could be obligatory to sell these goods in order to provide food, drink, clothing and shelter for those who lack these things.

He suggests that the church herself must guard against the dangers of consumerism which suggests that having is more important than being.
Justice in the World also contains some very strong teaching on this subject. The synod of bishops calls for all Christians to examine their lifestyles and urges all to ask "whether our lifestyle exemplifies that sparingness with regard to consumption which we preach to others as necessary in order that so many millions of hungry people throughout the world may be fed."
This has consequences then for both the institutional church as well as the members of the church. In both cases lifestyle simplicity is indicated.
10. *The Challenge of Peace,* para. 191.
    False.
Although some church spokespersons do suggest unilateral disarmament as a strategy for end-

ing the nuclear arms race, official Roman Catholic social teaching calls for bilateral or in fact multilateral disarmament. Thus, in accordance with the Vatican's stated position on this, *The Challenge of Peace* called for "immediate, bilateral, verifiable agreements to halt the testing, production, and deployment of new nuclear weapons systems."
When the pastoral letter was adopted, the U.S. bishops carefully stayed away from endorsing unilateral disarmament. While they did support independent initiatives on the part of the superpowers, the substantive actions which they supported were bilateral in nature.

LECTURE OUTLINE

Overview of Catholic Social Teaching

This is a very brief summary that simply contextualizes the points raised in the test within the broader framework of modern Catholic social teaching.

I. List of Document Names, Dates and Authors

The leader should have the following list on newsprint, and simply point to it noting the significant bases these offer for social ministry today.

1891 *Rerum Novarum*—Leo XIII
1931 *Quadragesimo Anno*—Pius XI
1961 *Mater et Magistra*—John XXIII
1963 *Pacem in Terris*—John XXIII
1965 *Pastoral Constitution on the Church in the Modern World*—Vatican II
1967 *Populorum Progressio*—Paul VI
1968 *Humanae Vitae*—Paul VI
1971 *Justice in the World*—Second Synod of Bishops
1979 *Redemptor Hominis*—John Paul II
1981 *Laborem Exercens*—John Paul II
1988 *Sollicitudo Rei Socialis*—John Paul II
1983 *Challenge of Peace*—U.S. Bishops
1986 *Economic Justice for All*—U.S. Bishops

II. Nature of the Teaching

The Nature of this Teaching

The U.S. bishops have taken giant steps in the 1980s to make this teaching known in the United

States. Two landmark pastoral letters, *The Challenge of Peace* and *Economic Justice for All* have applied the principles of Catholic social teaching to the American scene. In so doing, they have stirred up considerable interest in what some have called the church's best kept secret.

A question frequently arises regarding the nature of this teaching. In summarizing a response to such a question, the following points can be helpful.

First, Catholics rely on various sources for understanding, developing, and living their faith. Two primary sources are scripture and tradition. The teaching here fits into this second category.

Second, tradition can be seen to have various levels of authority. Highest is the infallible pronouncement, which has been used only once—in 1950 to establish the doctrine of the Assumption. The social teaching referred to in this test fit at the next level—encyclicals, synodal documents, and conciliar pronouncements.

Third, this teaching applies the Christian's faith as it has developed in the Roman Catholic tradition to the social concerns of our day, and the intent is obviously for Catholics to try and apply it in their lives. A useful dichotomy found in both *The Challenge of Peace* and *Economic Justice for All* distinguishes between moral principles and prudential judgments. Principles such as the prohibition against killing the innocent in war or, on a different plane, the right of workers to organize are inviolable. Judgments made that relate these and other principles to the real-life situations people face, however, are subject to differences of opinion.

Finally, John Coleman's description of the nature of these prudential judgments offers a concise and helpful guide to the nature of this teaching. Coleman writes,

The social teaching of the Church is an instance of authoritative but non-infallible teaching. As such it can only enjoy presumptive truth. The historical and contingent nature of a theology of culture and society means that much of social teaching is, in principle, reformable. The faithful are called to respond to the Church's social teaching with seriousness and assent as to its presumptive truth unless they have strong and urgent reasons to doubt its wisdom. For it is always possible, under definite conditions, to dissent from the Church's social teaching on specific issues and remain a Catholic in good standing. Such dissent would depend on both the careful study of the issue and prayerful discernment of the Gospel, the thrust of Catholic social teaching, and the community of those most faithful and sensitive to justice issues in the Church. Such dissent *in* the Church will be *for* the Church when it is rooted in the mission toward justice which is the Church's own.[1]

III. The Church's Mission

Briefly described, the mission of the church can be said to be threefold. The following diagram on newsprint can help people visualize it.

KERYGMA

Preach The Good News

KOINONIA   **DIAKONIA**

community   service

The social teaching, and the work of social ministry organizations is located, strictly speaking, in Diakonia. All three aspects of this mission must be present, however, for the church to be an authentic embodiment of the church of Jesus Christ.

This image of the church's mission serves a couple of purposes. First, it establishes the fundamental nature of the church's social mission. The social mission of the church does not represent an appendage added on after the roof is repaired and the principal is hired. Nor does it stand as a strategy of pre-evangelization. It has an integrity and significance that is irrefutable in our tradition.

At the same time, this image of the threefold mission qualifies the social mission. It is not all that the church should be about; it is only part of it. Reducing the church's activity to its social ministry would likewise be wrong.

Finally, the church exists to fulfill its mission. Liturgy, prayer, sacraments, and the church's institutional life can be said to exist not for themselves, but for the purpose of enabling the church, i.e., the people of God, to perform this threefold mission.

6. Exercise: Leadership Qualities: 30 min.

The purpose of this exercise is multifold. On its most superficial level, it engages the group in

1. John Coleman, *An American Strategic Theology,* New York: Paulist Press, 1982.

thinking about leadership and deciding individually what attributes one connects with leadership. At the same time, it gives the group its first task and an experience of group process and decision-making, all within a specific timeframe. In introducing the exercise, the facilitator relates only the first purpose. *Handout 1D* is used.

The Process

A. Completing the Form: 5 min.

Individuals follow the instructions on the top of *Handout 1D*. They have five minutes to complete this first phase of the exercise.

B. Small Group Meetings: 10 min.

Participants break into smaller groups of 5–8 persons, in separate rooms if possible. Each group must decide which *three* characteristics they consider to be most essential for a good leader to possess. The leader should not offer an answer if asked, "How do you want us to decide?" Each group will determine that. They have no more than 10 minutes to finish the exercise.

C. Debriefing: 10–15 min.

Debriefing begins with each group reporting its conclusions, and the leader's posting them on newsprint. The following questions can then stimulate a discussion of the exercise.

—Do you all agree that the 3 qualities that your group chose are the most important?
—How did you feel about the process used by the group to decide?
—What was the process? (If it wasn't already stated.)
—Did anyone feel excluded or unheard?

In closing the following points are important to note:

—It is important to reflect on how we do things; often it can be as important as what we do.
—Not listening to minority opinions carefully can cause problems for the group's dynamic. Problems can be sublimated only to appear in a more critical form later. Also, these opinions are likely to have some positive

aspects that the group should extract and make its own.
—Time limits are important. Questions like the one the group considered could be discussed for hours. Later the group will have many important tasks to accomplish at their meetings. It is important to accomplish them in an agreed upon fashion, and in a reasonable timeframe.

7. Break: 10 min.

Extending the break beyond the alloted ten minutes will throw off the schedule. The leaders must therefore attend to limiting the break accordingly. The hosts should make refreshments available, and a team member can check on preparedness so as not to delay the session.

8. Exercise: Looking Ahead: 30 min.

This activity leads participants to begin to consider social concerns that could be addressed by the Social Ministry Organization (SMO), and it provides an introduction to the two fundamental aspects of social ministry, social service and social action.

The Process

A. Setting Up: 10 min.

Dividing participants into groups of 6–8 people and keeping parish groups together when possible, the leader instructs the group to fantasize that the date is one year from now. S/he invites them to review their imaginary year together as a committee, and to list all of the Social Ministry Organization's achievements. It helps to stress the fantasy dimension of this exercise, and to encourage the groups to embellish freely and imagine wildly.

B. Debriefing: 10 min.

As each group announces its accomplishments, the facilitator will list the items on newsprint in one of three columns. In one column, s/he places those involvements that would fit under social service; under the second all that would correspond to social action are posted, and in the third column any other items are put. The latter column could include activities that would be extraneous to the work of a social ministry committee, or items that may have to do with the maintenance of the group, such as adding members or increasing parishioner involvement in the committee's work.

Do not reveal at this time why you are placing the actions in different columns.

Examples:

Column 1	Column 2	Column 3
Collect Food in the Parish	Write to Congress on a pressing issue	Hold Bible study classes
Visit the homebound	Get a traffic light installed at a busy intersection	Double committee membership

C. Lecture: Social Ministry: 10 min.

The leader now refers to *Handout 1E*. S/he points out that social ministry, the work done by the parish SMO, can be regarded as having two sides and that the various actions of the groups were listed as they were to correspond to them.

It frequently happens that the service list is much longer than the action list, but it is unusual for a group not to identify some of each. Harry Fagan, the author of *Empowerment* and a veteran Catholic social action leader, uses a version of the following story to illustrate these two components of social ministry.

One day, a missionary was praying by the river near the village where he lived. Suddenly, he noticed some bodies floating down the river. He pulled them out, found they were all dead, and gave them a Christian burial. The next day, more bodies came down the river; this time some were still alive. With the help of the villagers, he buried the dead, and nursed the survivors back to health. This continued to be a daily occurrence, and the whole village became caught up with the busy-ness of taking care of these people. They became so busy, in fact, that no one stopped and asked the question: "What's going on at the top of the river?"

The bodies floating down the river, the effects of some problem, needed to be helped, but it is, in the final analysis, necessary to discover why—the cause of the problem—they were coming down in

the first place. Consequently, both elements need to be on the committee's agenda.

The interconnectedness of these two elements can be seen in one of the U.S. Catholic Church's most visible social ministry organizations. Catholic Charities USA utilizes these basic concepts in defining its goals. Specifically, Charities is involved in convening, direct service, and advocacy. Convening brings people together, and in the case of social ministry, it is done to become familiar with the ways people in a particular community are hurting. Direct service, like pulling bodies from the river, responds to the immediate problem with aid. Advocacy involves speaking out and organizing to uproot the causes of social problems.

9. *Prayer: 15 min.*

Handout 1F contains the outline of the prayer service. Its theme is "Compassion," a spiritual quality which all involved in social ministry must pray constantly for.

Before beginning the prayer, the leader should create an environment for it. Setting up a table with a Bible and a candle would be sufficient. Whatever precise means are used, special arrangements for prayer during this and every session will help focus the group on this most important aspect of the ministry.

To begin this prayer, the leader should help the group center on the idea of compassion. Background music could be used to good effect as the leader elaborates on the three components of compassion that are noted on the prayer sheet.

At the time of petitions, the leader should be comfortable with silence if few speak. There will be other times during the process when participants will offer intercessions, and allowing the silence now can help people open up later.

10. *Preparation for Session II: 5 min.*

Handout 1G delineates the steps needed to prepare for Session II. Emphasis should again be placed on the importance of each person preparing for upcoming sessions. It will influence both the level at which each person will enjoy the program, and the potential benefit that the training program will have for the committee.

SESSION I—HANDOUT 1A

To help you begin to focus your thinking on social ministry, and on some of the topics this program covers, complete these statements with your own thoughts. This is for your eyes only so you need not hold back.

When I hear "social ministry," I think:

I feel most helpful to others when:

I think poor people should be able to:

I would consider it risky if my committee decided to:

My opinion of public assistance programs (welfare, food stamps) is:

Justice means:

God calls us to:

If I could change one thing in the world, it would be:

Something I really believe in is:

Charity means:

My faith helps me to:

The injustice I see in my community that needs attention is:

SESSION I—HANDOUT 1B

Social Ministry Training Program

Goal: To facilitate effective parish-based social ministry through a process of committee formation.

Methods: A variety of techniques, including lecture, discussion, and group work will be used to assist participants in familiarizing themselves with the THEOLOGY, SPIRITUALITY, and SKILLS that support parish social ministry. Preparation for and participation in each session's activities are of central importance. Presentations and lectures serve only to deepen and in some cases clarify the knowledge gained from the effort of each participant.

Six Session Overview

Session 1: Catholic Social Teaching Overview
            Expectations of Leaders
            Scope of Social Ministry
            Prayer

Session 2: Scriptural Basis of Social Concern
            Group Process
            Prayer

Session 3: Church Social Teaching I
            Leadership Functions
            Conflict Resolution
            Prayer

Session 4: Church Social Teaching II
            Keys to Social Reform
            Identifying Problems
            Prayer

Session 5: Selecting Priorities
            Prayer

Session 6: Task Force Meetings
            Social Ministry Committee Relationships
            Theology/Spirituality Summary
            Prayer

SESSION I—HANDOUT 1C

The Catholic Church Teaches

Directions: Circle T (true) or F (false) depending on what you believe is Catholic teaching. All answers are drawn from major church documents.

1. T F   Peacemaking is a good thing for Christians to do, but it is not a requirement of our faith.
2. T F   Each person has the right to security in the event of unemployment, old age or disability.
3. T F   The world's rich nations are morally obligated to give of their resources to assist poor nations.
4. T F   The split between the faith we profess and our daily lives is one of the most serious errors of our age.
5. T F   If a society fails to provide enough jobs for its workers, government has no responsibility to pick up the slack.
6. T F   From a biblical perspective the justice of a community or nation is measured by how it treats the poorest, most powerless members.
7. T F   The church supports, in all conditions, the right to private property.
8. T F   Counterpopulation warfare—i.e., tactics that target population centers for attack—is morally equal to murder.
9. T F   To be faithful to her mission, the church must be willing to give up some of her wealth and put it at the disposal of the poor.
10. T F   Unilateral disarmament is the church's suggested approach to the nuclear arms race.

Leadership Qualities

Choose the five characteristics from the following list which you think are most needed to make a good leader.

Responsible	_____
Outspoken	_____
Runs a meeting well	_____
Honest	_____
Gives direction	_____
Listens	_____
Friendly	_____
Uses common sense	_____
Initiates	_____
Coordinates	_____
Knows many people	_____
Makes decisions	_____
Knowledgeable	_____
Uses critical thinking	_____
Gets things done	_____

The Two Sides to Social Ministry

Side 1	**Response**	*Side 2*
Charity	**Response**	Justice
Effect	**Treats**	Cause
Service	**Provides**	Action

Examples of the Two Responses

Side 1	**Problem**	Side 2
Emergency food drive, and supporting soup kitchens.	**Hunger**	Lobbying for food stamps, WIC or other food programs.
Funding and staffing emergency shelters.	**Homelessness**	Working for construction of low-income housing.
Sponsoring a refugee family.	**Refugees**	Advocating Sanctuary or the rights of undocumented persons.

Additional Examples

Side 1	*Side 2*
Visiting shut-ins.	Community organizing.
Volunteer work.	Starting a food co-op.
Providing transportation.	Letter-writing to lawmakers.
Blood drives.	Forming a peacemaking group.
Emergency services.	Socially responsible investment.
Individual counseling.	

SESSION I—HANDOUT 1F

Prayer Service
Compassion

Centering on Compassion
    Solidarity: Experiencing Oneness
      Consolation: Entering another's Pain
       Comfort: Gaining new Strength

Reading: Exodus 22:20–24
Psalm Response: Psalm 34

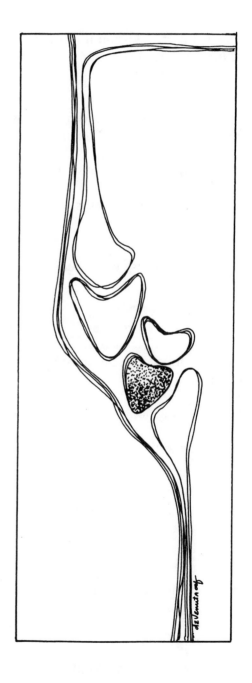

I. A cry goes up from the poor, and Yahweh hears,
    and helps the people in all their troubles.

II. How good Yahweh is—only taste and see!
     Happy the one whom Yahweh shelters.

I. The face of Yahweh frowns on evil ones,
     to wipe their memory from the earth;
    the eyes of Yahweh are turned toward the virtuous,
     Yahweh's ears to their cry.

II. They cry for help and Yahweh hears
     and rescues them from all their troubles;
    Yahweh is near to the brokenhearted,
     and helps those whose spirit is crushed.

All: Hardships in plenty beset the virtuous,
     but Yahweh rescues them from them all;
    Taking care of every bone,
     Yahweh will not let one be broken.

Reading: Luke 10:29–37

Shared reflection on scriptures

Petitions for those in need of our solidarity

  Response: Loving God, help us grow in our compassion.

Closing

29

SESSION I—HANDOUT 1G

Social Ministry Committee Training

Preparation for Session II

The first part of Session II will involve small group discussion on the scriptures noted below. In preparation for this, each person is asked to read the indicated passages, and reflect on the listed questions.

Old Testament

Read the following selections: Genesis 1:1–31, Exodus 3:1–20, Exodus 19:1–8, Exodus 20:2, Isaiah 52:1–53, Isaiah 58:1–12, Jeremiah 22:11–17.

While reading, look for answers to the following questions:

According to these readings, who is God, and what is God doing?

What does God ask of the people?

New Testament

Read the following selections: Luke 4:16–21, Matthew 25:31–46, Luke 6:46–49, Mark 1:14–15, and Philippians 2:1–11.

While reading, look for answers to the following questions:

According to these readings, who is Jesus, and what is his mission?

What does Jesus tell his followers to do?

Reflection Questions

What meaning do God's action of freeing Israel from slavery and Jesus's mission to free the oppressed have for you?

In what ways do these scriptures call you to deeper faith?

SESSION II

Introduction

Two principal activities fill most of the second session's agenda. An hour is allocated for "Confronting Scripture," a time for discussion and input on a series of scripture passages which the group has been asked to read and reflect upon during the time between sessions. Fifty minutes is scheduled for a structured exercise on group process skills. As with all sessions, time is also allotted for prayer, for a break, and for reviewing the preparation that must be done for the next meeting. One additional block of time goes for the group's choice of a transitional mission statement.

"Confronting Scripture" provides participants with their first opportunity in the process to focus with some depth on the faith basis for the church's social ministry. The selected passages feature the unmistakable concern for justice which characterizes our scriptural heritage. They make clear God's compassion for the oppressed, and Jesus' identification with the poor. They likewise highlight the unambiguous obligation that disciples have to serve Christ by serving the poor. "Confronting Scripture" intends to make very clear that the mission of this group is very much at the heart of the gospel.

"Confronting Scripture" also introduces the basic method that will be used during the organizing process for the theology sections. The process used invites individual reflection, facilitates small group discussion, and provides input to the group. This basic approach is replicated in the subsequent sessions.

While the section on scripture takes the group to some theological depth, the structured exercise "Choosing a Color" begins a deeper look at the group process skills needed for the group's growth and development. The exercise is one which people will remember long after the program. Its explicit purpose is to give participants the chance to play the roles that must be carried out in any successful group. It also serves to provide a good opportunity for group interaction, and has the effect of play. In simulating a meeting, "Choosing a Color" provides another opportunity for the group to experiment with decision making on matters of no real consequence.

In closing Session II, the group is asked to make a decision of some consequence. Specifically, the process suggests that they choose a provisional mission statement. Like any organization, parish social ministry organizations need to know specifically what their purpose is, but agreeing on the precise wording of a mission statement can be a long, laborious process. So, two mission statements—each the result of a real and protracted process—are offered for the group's consideration.

In making this choice, the people present will be integrating much of what has been covered in the first two sessions. The discussion will touch on theology and the understanding of how the church's social mission is animated at the parish level. It is a fitting summary to Session II.

SESSION II—SUGGESTED USE OF TIME

10 min.	1.	Prayer
60 min.	2.	Confronting Scripture
10 min.	3.	Break
55 min.	4.	Structured Experience: Choosing a Color
10 min.	5.	Mission Statement
5 min.	6.	Preparation for Session III

SESSION II: LEADER'S PLAN

Objectives

A. Content

1. Discuss the scriptural basis for Christian social concern.

2. Familiarize participants with the roles and functions important for positive group dynamic.

B. Process

1. Enable group to discuss among themselves the meaning and implications of the scripture readings, providing them with an experience of theological reflection.
2. Through a structured activity, the group will experience a meeting and engage in a decision-making process.

Preparation

The seating should be arranged in the same manner as in Session I, and an extra room should be available for small group activities. The easel and newsprint needs to be set up, and sign-up sheet and ID badges need to be available in an accessible place.

Equipment needed for the second session:

• Newsprint and Easel

Materials needed for session:

• Packet of handouts for Session II
• Bible
• "Choosing a Color" materials

Each trainer should complete a careful reading of the assigned texts for which she or he is responsible.

PROGRAM FOR SESSION II

1. Prayer: 10 min.

This session's prayer focuses on the responsibility we have to live in the world as Christ's disciples, and not to give in to the temptation of a piety that escapes from life's challenges.

In introducing the prayer the leader indicates that a reading, the opportunity for shared prayer, and the Lord's Prayer will comprise this evening's prayer, and that the theme is our responsibility to live our faith in our daily lives. *Handout 2A* contains the prayer service.

Again, the leader should be attentive to creating an environment for prayer.

2. Confronting Scripture: 60 min.

Participants will have read selections from the Old and New Testaments in preparation for this session. They will have considered questions on the content of the readings, and questions that provoke personal reflection. The leader will facilitate the three-part discussion that centers on the nature and identity of God, the mission of Jesus, and the responsibilities of the people of God.

This session intends to present a biblical theology of a loving, compassionate, liberating God whom all creation has as its source, and an understanding of Jesus Christ that shows his salvific mission to be one that incorporates concern for the integrated human person. Implicitly or explicitly, this will challenge notions of theological views that see God and Jesus in dualistic, pietistic, and thoroughly apolitical ways.

There are four segments to the process. First, the leader elicits responses to the objective questions, and posts them on newsprint. This is followed by small group discussion, plenary discussion, and input.

The Process

A. Listing of Responses: 10 min.

The facilitator will lead the consideration of the first set of questions by eliciting responses from the group. These questions are objective in nature, and lists can be compiled in response to each of the four questions. It is best to take one question at a time, but not refer the question to every reading. *Briefing Paper 2* contains detailed information on these answers. The leader should add any elements that are glaringly absent.

B. Small Group Discussion: 20 min.

The second step calls for small group discussion of the two reflection questions. The facilitator can make the transition to this section by asking how many people commonly regard God as a liberator

—there will likely be few or none—and how many understand Jesus' mission to be one of freeing the oppressed. It is important to point out that the Hebrews understood God as precisely that, and that Jesus, according to the evangelist Luke, announced that this, too, was his mission.

To allow for this discussion, the leader should:

- divide the large group into clusters of four to six people.
- ask that someone in each group assume the role of recorder.
- tell them they have fifteen minutes to discuss the questions among themselves, and that large group discussion will follow.

C. Plenary Discussion: 10 min.

The large group reassembles, and reporters from each group will offer highlights from their discussion. Others can also offer comments.

The facilitator may also focus the large group discussion on additional questions that could be posed to all. Examples might include:

- How has the reading, reflection and discussion expanded your understanding of God?
- Has this exercise focused on an aspect of the Bible that you had not dwelled on previously?

D. Lecture: 20 min.

The final step for this item is the lecture. An outline for it can be found in *Briefing Paper 2*. In *The Faith that Does Justice,* edited by John Haughey (Paulist Press, 1977), John Donahue authored an article that is an excellent bibliographical resource. The article, "Biblical Perspectives on Justice," can assist anyone leading this section.

BRIEFING PAPER 2: CONFRONTING SCRIPTURE

The consideration of scripture in the context of the Social Ministry Committee Training Program intends to illuminate the biblical basis for social concern. Methodologically, the participants are invited to examine several Old Testament and New Testament passages, consider in an objective

manner what is being said in them, and finally, reflect on the significance that the readings hold for their own lives.

In this segment of Session II, the leader first elicits responses to the objective questions, second, sets the stage for small group discussions on the subjective questions, and third, presents a lecture that elaborates on the scriptural basis for social concern and involvement. What follows in this briefing paper is a breakdown of key objective answers, and an outline and briefing for the lecture.

A. Responses to Questions

Consideration of the questions pertaining to who God is, who Jesus is, and what they ask of their followers is the first step in this process. There is no need to systematically proceed through this list with the group. Instead use it as a handy reference sheet to check that all major ideas have surfaced.

From left to right is the biblical citation, and principal answers to the questions from each.

Citation	Who God/Jesus is	Demands of Followers
Old Testament		
Gen. 1:1–31	Creator of all	Be stewards over creation
Ex. 3:1–20	Compassionate one/Liberator	Accept one's calling (Moses)
Ex. 19:1–8	Liberator	Obey God and keep the covenant
Ex. 20:2	Liberator (this is the explicit identity)	Keep the commandments
Is. 58:1–12	Compassionate one who cares especially for the oppressed	Be just. Worship without justice is rejected by God
Jer. 22:11–17	Same as Is. 58	Integrity, honesty, justice, mercy, compassion
Is. 52:13–Is. 53:12	Suffering Servant	

Citation	Who God/Jesus is	Demands of Followers
New Testament		
Lk. 4:16–21	Teacher, liberator	
Mk. 1:14–15	Prophet, announces the reign of God	Repent and believe
Mt. 25	King, judge, person in need	Feed the hungry, care for all needy people
Lk. 6:46–49	Lord and teacher	Hear the words and act on them
Phil. 2:1–11	Humble slave, Lord, God's equal	Be as Christ—a humble servant. Worship Jesus Christ

As the Leader's Plan indicates, participants will be asked to give answers to the questions. All of the above should arise. There will most assuredly be additional ones as well.

B. and C.—See leader's notes above.

D. Lecture

The Leader's Plan also notes that after this listing is complete, small groups will be formed to discuss the reflection questions. Following this, and the large group discussion, the following material can be used to present a lecture.

Lecture Outline

When starting the leader notes that the intention is not to "proof text," that is, s/he is not trying to justify some practice or condemn another. The Bible suits itself readily to abuse of this type, as virtually anything can be justified or condemned through selective references. The intention, on the other hand, is to expose a rich vein that runs throughout the Bible and implores us to be deeply concerned about our world.

SCRIPTURE OUTLINE

I. Who is God, and what does God ask of the people?

The readings that the program participants have done depict a God who is the source of all creation, and the ultimate paradigm of justice. As the latter, Yahweh is understood by Israel as being the One who liberated them from slavery, an action taken out of compassion for them. The covenant that they accepted subsequently mandated that they carry on God's liberating activity in history by compassionately responding to the cries of the widows, the orphans, and the strangers, i.e., the poor and powerless ones of that day. God descries their failure to do this through the prophets who called the nation to account, and warned the people of Israel to return to the covenant.

In these functions as Creator, Liberator, and Covenant-giver, God establishes sovereignty over all creation, and confirms an involvement and concern with the creation. A key point to emphasize is the this-worldly nature of the concern and involvement, and the concomitant mandate to the people to maintain God's example of justice through the institutions of their society.

The following elements can be integrated into the lecture:

A. God is Creator, Liberator and Covenant-giver.

B. God is compassionate, saying to Moses, "I have heard the cries of my people . . ."

C. God's identity vis-a-vis the Hebrews is unmistakable. "I, the Lord, am your God, who brought you out of the land of Egypt, that place of slavery." This identity recurs throughout the Old Testament. God is remembered and worshiped as such.

D. The covenant's implications for Israel were that the people were to follow the Lord's example in being just and compassionate; special care must be given to the widow, orphan, and stranger, the powerless ones of that time.

E. The prophets were sent to call the people back to fidelity to the covenant. Both the Isaiah 58 and Jeremiah 22 readings are stirring rejoinders to a people who had wandered from the covenant's precepts. The former shows an angry God who rejects worship from a nation that is unjust, the latter includes the profound implication that it is only those who do justice who can genuinely claim to know the Lord.

F. The suffering servant was a role assumed by Jesus, and this can provide the transition into consideration of the New Testament readings. The depth of God's compassion, and the continuing role of God in history, demonstrated by the incarnation, can be shown through this reading.

II.   Who is Jesus and what does he ask of his followers?

As with the Old Testament readings, these New Testament selections emphasize the biblical sources of contemporary social concern. Continuity with the Old Testament is evident in the transitional selection from Isaiah 52, and the Lucan selection where Jesus announces his mission with words from Isaiah 61. Jesus is therefore situated in the tradition of the Hebrew prophets. Being the Son of God, he incarnates the compassion and concern of God and carries on God's liberating activity through the offer of a new covenant.

Again, as with the consideration of God, it is important to accent Jesus' concern for this-worldly affairs. In so doing, the leader balances the frequent tendency to spiritualism. The readings show Jesus to be concerned about people and their situations in life, while calling his followers to be similarly concerned.

The following points can be included in the lecture:

A. Jesus' identity is the suffering servant (Is. 52), the humble servant/slave (Phil. 2), and the King incarnate in the poor (Mt. 25).

B. Jesus' mission is to proclaim the reign of God, and call people to repentance (Mk. 1). This is made more explicit in the Lucan passage where it includes bringing good news to the poor, and freedom to the oppressed.

C. Our mission, according to these readings, is to obey the covenant (Lk. 6), feed the hungry . . . (Mt. 25), and remove the cause of hunger . . . (Lk. 4). In both this and in Jesus' mission, emphasis should be placed on the this-worldly nature of the mission. Cautioning against a "spiritualizing" of these readings is a useful means of doing this.

D. A final point on the christology advanced here is useful. Some would make Jesus a political messiah, a revolutionary of sorts whose concern is only with the worldly. At the other pole is a thoroughly spiritualized Christ who presides from a throne far removed from the nitty-gritty of daily life. Neither interpretation is adequate.

The Jesus of the gospels clearly engaged compassionately the lives of the people he encountered. The manner of his execution, by crucifixion, was reserved for political criminals, and therefore it is plain to see that Rome perceived him as a political threat. Yet, Jesus also rejected any attempt to assume earthly power. A fitting conclusion to the lecture may be to suggest that Christ was political in a pious way, and pious in a political way. He was, contrary to the Greek dualism that has affected the understanding of Christ, concerned for the whole person, body and soul.

III.   Who are we?

Implicit in the demands of the followers of God and of Jesus is a certain understanding of the human person and human society. In brief, here are some of the anthropological conclusions one might draw from the Hebrew and Christian scriptures:

A. Human beings are created in the image and likeness of God, and as such each person is entitled to reverence.

B. Humanity can best be described as fallen but redeemed. One cannot escape the sinfulness that pervades human hearts and human society, a sign of our fallen state. Yet, our redemption allows us to be open to and to heed God's call to truth and righteousness. So it was that the prophets called Israel back to faithfulness to the covenant, and Jesus beckoned all who would listen to a life of love and concern for others.

C. People are intended to live in community. The obligations of the covenant were to be met by the entire community in its establishment and maintenance of structures and laws that approximated justice.

At the conclusion of the lecture, the leader refers the group to *Handout 2B* which lists a series of biblical citations that can be the source of further reflection and study on the scriptural basis for social concern.

3. *Break: 10 min.*

As in the first session, break should be no more than 10 minutes, and a team member should check to see that refreshments are prepared.

4. *"Choosing a Color": 55 min.*

This structured activity simulates a meeting. It exposes the group to the various roles and functions that are played out in a group, and it engages the group in a decision-making process. *Background Paper 2* contains an explanation of the complete activity.

The materials needed for the exercise are described in the background paper. There are three envelopes in the packet given to each group. Before beginning the activity, the facilitator must insure that the number of small envelopes in Envelope I corresponds to the number of people in the respective groups. Ordinarily there are ten small envelopes, but with fewer people, the appropriate number of items will have to be removed.

The Process

A. Introduction: 10 min.

Before starting the exercise, the leader will begin by noting that in every group there are certain roles that must be manifest within the group's dynamic in order for it to move effectively forward toward the attainment of its goals. In performing these functions, many of which come naturally to specific individuals, the various members of the group are participating as leaders. Specifically, the leader will point out and describe the following eight functions or roles. These roles, which should be posted on newsprint, and the brief descriptions are as follows:

1. *Information seeker:* asks for clarification of suggestions, requesting additional information or facts.
2. *Tension-reliever:* reduces intensity or potential for conflict by joking or jesting; puts tense situation in a larger context.
3. *Clarifier:* takes seemingly muddled ideas, and makes sense of them; tries to envision how a proposal might work if adopted.
4. *Gatekeeper:* tries to make it possible for an-

other member to make a contribution to the group by inviting someone who has not contributed to speak, or suggests limiting talking time so everyone will have a chance to be heard.
5. *Initiator:* proposes solutions, suggests new ideas, new definitions of the problem, new attack on the problem or new organization of material.
6. *Follower:* going along with the decisions of the group, thoughtfully accepting the ideas of others, serving as an audience during group discussion.
7. *Information-giver:* offering facts or generalizations, relating one's own experience to the group problem to illustrate points.
8. *Harmonizer:* shows relationships among various ideas or suggestions, tries to pull ideas and suggestions together.

After these are reviewed, the facilitator will tell participants that the next activity will give them the opportunity to become active in fulfilling one of these functions. The group ought to be encouraged to prepare themselves for a little acting as the roles they receive may not be natural for them to play.

B. The Structured Activity: 30 min.

Small groups of 7–10 persons will be formed, and an envelope containing all the materials for the exercise will be given to each group. As per the instructions in *Background Paper 2,* the envelope will be placed in the midst of each small group, and no further instructions will be given. One caveat to that, however, is that the facilitator should observe carefully during the beginning of the exercise, and intervene if the group begins to choose its color before opening the envelopes containing the roles. On their own, the group will complete the three phases of the activity.

C. Debriefing the Exercise: 10 min.

Debriefing. This will be a large group continuation of Phase III of the exercise when each group discussed questions about the behaviors that helped and hindered the group in accomplishing its task. Some other questions that could be asked when the whole group reassembles are:

- Did you feel capable of playing your role?
- Find out which two people were supposed to work to become the chairperson. Ask them to explain how they tried to accomplish their task. Did one of them succeed? Were others aware of what they were doing?
- Mention again the point made during the introductory remarks about shared leadership: that there are a variety of roles that are essential to group cohesion and success. Did it occur to anyone that they have leadership qualities of which they were not aware?

D. Handout 2C: 5 min.

In closing consideration of the exercise, the leader refers the group to *Handout 2C*: "Group Process Task and Maintenance Roles" and points out that the functions listed are divided into three categories. The first two categories correspond to the two general areas of Task Roles, and Group Building and Maintenance Roles. It can be said that these are two sides of the coin of effective group process. Without fulfillment of task roles nothing will be done, and without the other there will be no group to do anything. The third category are roles that serve both of these general areas.

Also included on this handout are descriptions of certain dysfunctional behavior.

In reviewing this handout, the leader doesn't need to read each one, or to elaborate in any detail. Simply point to the categories, indicate examples of each type, and encourage participants to review the lists after the session and consider what roles they typically would assume.

5. Mission Statement: 10 min.

The leader refers the group to *Handout 2D* which includes the mission statements of two parishes, pointing out that each statement includes both working to alleviate the effects, and to confront the causes of social problems.

Indicate that it will be important for each parish committee to articulate its own mission statement, but since that can be a difficult process, each group is being asked to accept one of these as a "Provisional Mission Statement." Minor changes can be made but each group is advised to

choose the one with which they are most comfortable.

After asking each parish group to choose the charter they prefer, the facilitator guides the discussion to its conclusion.

6. Preparation for Session III: 5 min.

In closing the session, the leader refers the group to *Handout 2E*, asking them to read it over, and inviting questions. It is important to make special mention of the assignment to identify problems, and to point out *Handout 2F*. This "Surveying Social Problems" is the first step in the group's determination of its action agenda.

Finally, the leader should again emphasize the importance of completing the assignments, admonishing that neither their participation nor their small group's deliberations will be as fruitful as it can be if they are not fully prepared.

BACKGROUND PAPER 2

"Choosing a Color"

This background paper provides the detailed instructions for the structured exercise "Choosing a Color."[1]

Goals

I. To explore behavioral responses to an ambiguous task.

II. To demonstrate the effects of shared leadership.

Group Size

Seven to ten participants. Several groups may be directed simultaneously.

---

1. This exercise is taken from *A Handbook of Structured Experiences for Human Relations Training*, Vol. 1, J. William Pfeiffer and John E. Jones, eds. (San Diego: University Associates, 1974), pp. 56–64. University Associates annually publishes excellent and varied resources relevant to group process issues.

Time Required

Approximately forty-five minutes

Materials

I. Prepare the following according to the Choosing a Color Envelopes Instruction Sheet:

1. Envelope 1: Directions for Phase I and seven to ten smaller envelopes, each containing an instruction card for an individual role player. (More specific instructions follow.)
2. Envelope 2: Directions for Phase II.
3. Envelope 3: Directions for Phase III.

II. Large envelope containing envelopes I, II, & III.

Physical Setting

Each group is seated in a circle.

Process

I. The facilitator discusses the concept of shared leadership. The following roles are explained:

1. Information seeker
2. Tension-reliever
3. Information-giver
4. Gatekeeper
5. Follower
6. Clarifier
7. Harmonizer
8. Initiator

II. The facilitator places the large envelope which contains envelopes I, II, and III in the center of the group, giving no further instructions or information. (The group must complete Phases I, II, and III by following directions in the envelopes.)

CHOOSING A COLOR ENVELOPES INSTRUCTION SHEET

The following instructions are written on the large envelope which contains envelopes I, II and III.

Instructions: Enclosed you will find three envelopes which contain directions for the phases of this group session. You are to open the envelope labeled I at once. Subsequent instructions will tell you when to open Envelopes II and III.

Envelope I holds a sheet of paper with the following group task instructions, and smaller envelopes each containing a role-player card.

Instructions for Group Task: Phase I
Time allowed: 15 minutes
Task: The group is to choose a color.

Special Instructions: Each member is to take one of the smaller envelopes from Envelope I and to follow individual instructions contained on the card in it.

Do not let anyone else see your instructions

After 15 minutes go on to the next envelope.

Instructions for Facilitator: How to Prepare Role-Player Cards

Envelope I holds smaller envelopes containing instructions for roles and positions that role players are to take. (Two of the instructions include special knowledge.)

If there are fewer than ten participants in the group, eliminate as many of the *last three roles* and positions as are necessary. There must be at least seven people in the groups. The information should be typed on cards. Then each card should be put in a small envelope.

Card #1
Role: Information seeker
Position: Support Blue

Card #2
Role: Tension-reliever
Position: Introduce the idea of a different color—orange

Card #3
Role: Clarifier
Position: Support Red

Card #4
Role: None
Position: None

(You have the special knowledge that the group is going to be asked to select a chairperson later in the exercise. You are to conduct yourself in such a manner that they will select you as chairperson.)

Card #5
Role: Gatekeeper
Position: None

Card #6
Role: Initiator
Position: Support Green

Card #7
Duplicate of card #4.

Card #8
Role: Follower
Position: Against Red.

Card #9
Role: Information-giver
Position: Against Blue.

Card #10
Role: Harmonizer
Position: Against Green.

Envelope II contains a sheet of paper with the following instructions:

Instructions for Group Task: Phase II
Time allowed: 5 minutes.
Task: You are to choose a group chairperson.

After the chairperson is chosen, go on to the next envelope.

Envelope III contains a sheet of paper with the following information:

Instructions for Group Task: Phase III
Time allowed: 10 minutes
Task: You are to discuss the process that emerged during the problem-solving phase of this group session.

Special Instructions: The chairperson will lead this discussion.
Sample questions:

1. What behaviors helped the group accomplish its task?
2. What behaviors hindered the group?

(After 10 minutes return the materials to their respective envelopes)

SESSION II—HANDOUT 2A

Prayer Service
Theme: Our Responsibility in This World

Call to Prayer

Readings from Church Social Teaching

Pastoral Constitution on the Church in the Modern World, Vatican II.

"This Council exhorts Christians, as citizens of two cities, to strive to discharge their earthly duties conscientiously and in response to the gospel spirit. They are mistaken who, knowing that we have here no abiding city but seek one which is to come, think that they may therefore shirk their earthly responsibilities. For they are forgetting that by the faith itself they are more than ever obliged to measure up to these duties, each according to their proper vocation."

On Social Concern, John Paul II, 1987.

"It is appropriate to emphasize the preeminent role that belongs to the laity, both men and women. . . . It is their task to animate temporal realities with Christian commitment, by which they show that they are witnesses and agents of peace and justice."

Silent Reflection

How does this call affect you? Your parish? How are we challenged by it?

Shared Reflection

Petitions

Response: Loving God, help us take on our responsibility.

The Lord's Prayer

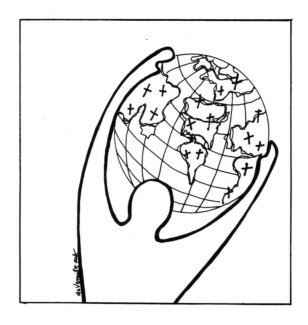

Scripture References

The following list of scriptural citations are samples of passages from the Old and New Testaments that pertain to justice. They can serve the group as resources for prayer, as well as for further study of the biblical bases for social concern.

Old Testament
Gen. 4:9–10
Ex. 3:1–20
Ex. 22:20–24
Lev. 25:23–38
Dt. 15:4
Dt. 24:17–22
Dt. 30
Ps. 72
Ps. 82
Ps. 103
Is. 1:10–28
Is. 2:1–5
Is. 5:8–9
Is. 32:16–17
Is. 42:1–4
Is. 58:1–12
Is. 61:1–2
Jer. 6:13–16
Jer. 22:13–16

Amos 5:14–15
Amos 5:21–24
Amos 8:4–7
New Testament
Mt. 5:1–12
Mt. 6:19–34
Mt. 11:2–6
Mt. 16:32–38
Mt. 20:20–28
Mt. 23:23
Mt. 25:31–46
Mt. 26:16–20
Mk. 8:31–38
Mk. 10:13–16
Mk. 10:17–27
Mk. 10:35–45
Lk. 1:46–55
Lk. 3:10–18
Lk. 4:16–20
Lk. 6:20–26

Lk. 10:25–37
Lk. 12:13–21
Lk. 15:1–3
Lk. 16:19–31
Lk. 22:24–27
Jn. 10:1–18
Jn. 13:1–15
Jn. 13:34–35
Jn. 14:10–17
Acts 2:43–47
Acts 4:32–35
Acts 6:1–6
Acts 16:16–24
Rom. 14:17–19
1 Cor. 13
2 Cor. 8:1–15
Jas. 2:14–24
Rev. 21:1–4

Group Process Task and Maintenance Roles

For any group, regardless of its purpose, to work effectively certain roles must be played by its members. The lists below cover several categories of roles. Most occur quite naturally. Depending on a particular group, others may need to be given special focus. One way or another all should be carried out in the group.

A. TASK ROLES (functions required in selecting and carrying out a group task).

1. INITIATING ACTIVITY: getting things started, proposing solutions, suggesting new ideas, or defining the problem in a new way.
2. SEEKING (GIVING) INFORMATION: asking for (offering clarification of) suggestions, requesting (giving) more information on a subject.
3. SEEKING (GIVING) OPINION: soliciting (stating) an opinion or a belief; seeking (giving) clarification of values or ideas.
4. ELABORATING: clarifying, giving examples or developing meanings; trying to envision how a proposal might work if adopted.
5. COORDINATING: showing relationships among various ideas or suggestions, trying to pull ideas and suggestions together, trying to draw together disparate activities.
6. SUMMARIZING: pulling together related ideas or suggestions, restating suggestions after the group has discussed them.

B. GROUP BUILDING AND MAINTENANCE ROLES (functions required in strengthening and maintaining group life and activities).

1. ENCOURAGING: being friendly, warm, responsive to others, praising others and their ideas, accepting others' contributions.
2. GATEKEEPING: inviting quiet members to offer their views, or suggesting limiting speaking time so all might contribute.
3. STANDARD SETTING: expressing standards for the group as it makes decisions, reminding group of its mission and need to focus on it.
4. FOLLOWING: going along with the decisions of the group, thoughtfully accepting the ideas of others.
5. EXPRESSING GROUP FEELING: summarizing what group feeling is on a topic being considered.

C. GROUP TASK AND MAINTENANCE ROLES (serves both ends).

1. EVALUATING: submitting group decisions or actions to comparison with group standards or goals.
2. DIAGNOSING: determining sources of difficulties with the group, and suggesting steps to overcome them.
3. TESTING FOR CONSENSUS: testing group opinion to see if a consensus is near; using trial balloons to check group's opinion.

4. MEDIATING: harmonizing, conciliating differences in points of view, making compromise solutions.
5. RELIEVING TENSION: breaking intensity with humor or putting a tense matter in a broader context.

D. TYPES OF NONFUNCTIONAL BEHAVIOR (counterproductive actions).

1. BEING AGGRESSIVE: working for status by criticizing others, deflating the ego or status of others.
2. BLOCKING: interfering with the progress of a group by going off on a tangent, arguing too much, or not listening.
3. SELF-CONFESSING: using the group as a sounding board for matters not related to the group.
4. COMPETING: vying with others to produce the best ideas, talk the most, gain the leader's favor.
5. SPECIAL PLEADING: introducing or supporting suggestions related to one's own pet concerns or philosophies.
6. HORSING AROUND: inappropriate clowning, joking or mimicking that disrupts the group's work.
7. WITHDRAWAL: acting indifferent or passive, resorting to formality, whispering to others, wandering from the subject.

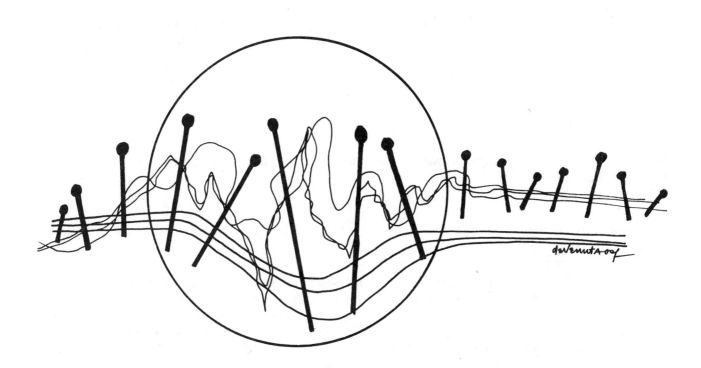

Social Ministry Committee Mission Statements

One of the following "mission statements" can serve a committee on an ad hoc basis until such time as the group crafts its own. Both statements were developed by existing social ministry committees.

Statement 1

"Whatever you do
For one of these
The least of my sisters and brothers,
You did it for me."
(Matthew 25)

The purpose of the committee is to help the people of the parish meet the social needs of our sisters and brothers as Christ has asked us.

This is to be accomplished by researching the needs, and organizing or supporting programs both to remedy the effects of social problems and to remove the basic causes of the problems through the prayers and actions of the parish community.

Membership is open to all interested in furthering the purpose of this committee.

Statement 2

Purpose: To stimulate the parish's awareness of human social needs and to develop effective responses to these needs.
Definition of Committee Task:

1. To educate ourselves and the parish community through dialogue and critical Christian reflection on the social mission of the church.
2. To promote the church's social mission by:
   a. working for and calling the parish to work for structural and systemic changes in the economic, social and political order that promote the values of the reign of God.
   b. calling forth the resources of the parish community to meet the needs of the world community (e.g., food collections, Operation Rice Bowl, Campaign for Human Development.)
   c. empowering oppressed people by promoting self-help projects.
3. To network with other groups in the parish and community.

SESSION II—HANDOUT 2E

Social Ministry Organizing Process

Preparation for Session III

To Campaign for Justice

This booklet contains the "Magna Carta" of church teaching on justice. The Vatican statement that has gained this distinction is entitled *Justice in the World*. Appendix I (pp. 33–52) contains the full text of the 1971 Synod of Bishops statement. A paraphrased version can be found on pp. 9–28.

To prepare for Session III read one of these versions of the document. Note that paragraph numbers correspond in each version, and a comparative reading can assist the reader in gaining insight into the document.

While reading, reflect on the following questions:

a. What is *Justice in the World* saying to you as a Catholic living in the United States?

b. According to *Justice in the World,* how is the church to fulfill its mission to work for justice? What steps should be taken? Methods used?

Identifying Problems

In Session IV participants will be asked to identify one problem which they think the group ought to address. To begin preparation for that step, conduct your own informal surveying of community, national or world problems that may be suitable subjects of the committee's concern.

Handout 2F provides a questionnaire that can guide you in your survey.

Surveying Social Problems

A problem is a generalized concern that affects a number of people. Identifying problems that a Social Ministry Committee can and should address provides the starting point for a group's work. The questions that follow are intended to help open the door for this step.

1. During the next week be attentive to the task of identifying problems when you:
   Drive through the parish or community—
   What problems present themselves?:

   Read the newspaper—

   Watch TV Newscasts—

2. Name groups in your parish who are "at risk" or are marginalized in some way (e.g., Youth, Elderly, Single-parent families, Unemployed, etc.).

3. Name any specific problems which the groups named in #2 encounter.

4. Which three problems that you have identified in questions 1 and 3 would you find most important and suitable for your committee to address?

   1.

   2.

   3.

SESSION III

SESSION 4

Introduction

Session III continues the mix of theology and group process that set the pattern in the previous meeting. It also further sets the stage for the group's agenda setting.

This time the theology focuses on Catholic social teaching. Participants will have familiarized themselves with *Justice in the World,* the 1971 Second Synod of Bishops statement. The process used to deal with it is very similar to what occurred with "Confronting Scripture" in Session II.

Two important topics related to group process receive attention in this session, "Leadership Qualities" and "Conflict Resolution." Time constraints limit them to little more than an introduction of each, but a liberal number of handouts provide enduring resources for the participants.

This session also moves the group closer to defining its action agenda. A central step in this process is the identification of problems that the committee and parish might address. In preparation for Session II, participants were asked to use *Handout 2F* to begin this. During the recap that opens Session III, the group has the chance to reveal some of the problems they have noticed. For Session IV they will be asked to make a brief presentation on one problem which they want to urge the group to adopt as a priority.

Related to this is a model of committee operation presented in the Leadership Qualities segment. This model suggests a framework for the committee that includes establishing task forces to work on specific problems, and that identifies several functions that would fall to a parish's social ministry committee.

Session III also engages the group in the selection of the criteria it will use in choosing the problems it will address.

SESSION III—SUGGESTED USE OF TIME

10 min.	1.	Prayer
15 min.	2.	Recap/Feedback
50 min.	3.	*Justice in the World*
10 min.	4.	Break
25 min.	5.	Leadership Functions
25 min.	6.	Conflict Resolution
15 min.	7.	Prioritizing Criteria
5 min.	8.	Preparation for Session IV

SESSION III: LEADER'S PLAN

Objectives

A. Content

1. Examine the document *Justice in the World.*
2. Consider group leadership functions.
3. Review conflict resolution principles.
4. Present criteria for prioritizing.

B. Process

1. Involve participants in theological reflection.
2. Presentations and review of materials on Leadership Functions and Conflict Resolution.

Preparation

Again, facilitators should have facilities arranged properly, and have ID badges and sign-up sheet available.

Equipment needed for third session:

- newsprint and easel
- masking tape.

Materials needed for session:

- packet of handouts
- copies of *This Land is Home to Me.*

Solid familiarity with the sections that will be covered during the session is required for each leader in their respective areas of responsibility. Each facilitator must be certain to have studied handouts, and background materials for your respective section.

PROGRAM FOR SESSION III

1. Prayer: 10 min.

This session's prayer focuses on the link between the church's worship and sacraments and the mission to work for justice.

Handout 3A will be used for the prayer.

As with previous sessions, leaders should endeavor to create an environment for prayer.

2. Recap/Feedback/Problem Identification: 15 min.

The facilitator will begin the session by briefly recapping what has been covered thus far, and contextualizing it with where the program is leading. Additionally, the group was asked to begin the process of identifying problems that they might address, and this time provides the opportunity to surface the results of their initial efforts.

Regarding the recap, the following points should be made:

- Regarding theology, point out that an overview of social teaching was done through the first session's pre-test, and an examination of the scriptural basis was accomplished last week. This session will begin the consideration of some specific documents in the body of Catholic social teaching.
- Pertaining to group process, recall "Choosing a Color" and the Leadership Qualities exercise, and indicate that tonight some specific functions of leadership will be explored.
- Concerning social action skills, indicate that the group began, through its assignment for this week, the process that will be given much attention during the next four sessions.

After the recap, offer participants an opportunity to offer any feedback that they might have at this point in the program. Is it meeting expectations? Are the preparations too burdensome? Etc.

On the preparations question, if as often is the case, some regard it as heavy, the leader should acknowledge their concern. But, also take the opportunity to suggest that while you are aware that much is being asked for, there is nothing superfluous in the assignments. In addition, point out that their preparation for Session III involved the heaviest work, and that it is all downhill from here. Encourage people to continue to do their best to complete the preparation each week.

Finally, before beginning the review of *Justice in the World,* survey the group to learn what kind of problems they identified in preparation for this session. List some on newsprint, and get a good taste of the problems people have noticed.

This is an important step. It is essential for the group members to take very seriously the task of identifying problems, for the quality of their action agenda will depend upon this initiative.

3. Justice in the World: 50 min.

To prepare for this section, the group was asked to read *Justice in the World,* and to reflect on two focus questions. This assignment and this section give participants the opportunity to read, reflect on, and discuss what many consider the Magna Carta for Catholic involvement in the transformation of the world. Besides its doctrinal significance, symbolized by the quotation, "Action on behalf of justice . . . fully appears to us to be a constitutive dimension of the preaching of the Gospel," it is the most readable example of Vatican social teaching.

Like Session II's treatment of scripture, the process that will be used possesses significance for the group that extends beyond the content of the document itself. The process gives participants the chance to discuss the implications of the teaching, and the teaching itself before being encumbered by "expert" commentary. By the end of the program, such experiences will hopefully have enabled the group to perceive its ability to continue such study of scripture and social teaching even though no "expert" may be available.

The Process

A. Small Group Discussions: 15 min.

The leader begins by dividing people into groups of 6–8 people. The small groups are then directed to gather in the various locations available, and to spend the next fifteen minutes discussing the focus questions. Each group should appoint a recorder who will be responsible to report back to the larger group in the discussion that will follow.

During the discussion period, the leader can circulate unobtrusively among the groups in order to gain a sense of the conversations that are occurring.

B. Plenary Discussion: 15 min.

The leader reconvenes the large group, and the discussion continues with recorders from each group summarizing their respective discussions. Key concepts are placed on newsprint. Subsequently, others are invited to add to the recorders' summaries.

Also, participants are asked at this point if questions arose during their reading or discussion which have not yet been answered satisfactorily. The leader responds to them while maintaining consciousness of the time, and the fact that some of them may be answered during the lecture that follows.

C. Lecture: 20 min.

The transition can be made by pointing to *Handout 3B* which shows the See, Judge, Act method of the document, and outlines the key points made in each section. *Briefing Paper 3A* follows with an outline and description for this lecture.

BRIEFING PAPER 3A: LECTURE ON *JUSTICE IN THE WORLD*

The lecture on *Justice in the World* provides the leader responsible for this section with a framework and notes for the lecture. The leader should feel free to adapt it in such a way as to be comfortable with it and to present it in that way. Elaborations and anecdotes to the material would be helpful to give the presentation vitality.

When preparing this lecture, a timed rehearsal will assist in the important task of limiting the comments to the twenty minutes allotted for it.

LECTURE ON *JUSTICE IN THE WORLD*

I. Document's Methodology and Content

See, Judge, Act: a framework for social teaching and action (refer to *Handout 3B*.)

Europe's Catholic Action Movement adopted this method in the 1930s, and it is the approach used in much of the post-Vatican II social teaching. The Council's Pastoral Constitution on the Church in the Modern World, Paul VI's *On the Development of Peoples,* and all the documents we will study in this course employ it. It likewise is familiar to all who have been involved in the Catholic Family Movement.

A. What Is Seen (Refer to the first column of the handout)

The synod looked at the world through the eyes of church people who were eager to tune in to the sufferings of the poor. In the introduction to the document, they echo the voice of God when first addressing Moses. They write:

"Listening to the cry of those who suffer violence and are oppressed by unjust systems and structures, and hearing the appeal of a world that by its perversity contradicts the plan of its Creator, we have shared our awareness of the church's vocation to be present in the heart of the world by proclaiming the Good News to the poor, freedom to the oppressed and joy to the afflicted." (paragraph 5)

This perspective is important to emphasize. It is different from the view of the corporate or political elite. As such it conditions what they see. The following points summarize what they observe:

1. *Crisis in Universal Solidarity:* Here the bishops identify some of the problems they perceive while noting that the positive ingredients are present as well. The latter can serve as the basis for change. The handout indicates the key points.
2. *Right to Development:* The right to development incorporates all the human rights that the church's mission mandates it defend. It can be described simply as the right of each person to determine one's own future—to be

subjects or persons as opposed to objects or things.

They also note that this calls for full participation in economic, social, and political matters. Structures that deny this right to participation are sinful. Moving toward this kind of participation is a key element in the church's pastoral response.

3. *Voiceless Injustices:* As Jesus said he could be found in the poor (Matthew 25), the bishops here make the concerns of the poorest, most powerless people their own concerns. The handout lists these groups of persons.

B. How Is it Judged (Handout's second column.)

The bishops begin this section by stating unequivocally that injustice is a sin. Dwell on the implications of this. Sin, consequently, is not only personal, it is also social. The implication for Catholics is that just as we are called to reform our personal lives by turning away from sin, we are also obligated to reform the social structures that perpetrate injustice. To fail to do so is to cooperate with the sin, and thus to participate in the sin.

John Paul II sheds additional light on this subject with his reference to "structures of sin" in his 1987 encyclical *On Social Concern.* The all-consuming quest for profit and thirst for power are the two principal sins he dwells upon in his encyclical.

1. *Saving Justice of God through Christ.* Refer again to the echo of God's words to Moses. In this section of the document, the synod explains the scriptural and theological basis that it utilizes in evaluating the world order. Refer to the items listed on the handout, and point out the similarity between this and the context of last session's discussion on scripture. Emphasize the significance of working for this-worldly liberation as demonstrated in paragraph 35 where the bishops write:

> The mission of preaching the gospel dictates at the present time that we should dedicate ourselves to the liberation of the human person even in his present existence in the world. For unless the Christian message of love and justice shows its effectiveness through action in the cause of

justice in the world, it will only with difficulty gain credibility with the people of our times.

2. *Mission of the Church hierarchy and Christians.* Again refer to the handout, and the items listed. Emphasis should be placed on the church's mission to defend and promote human dignity and human rights, and that Christians should live in the world under the influence of the gospel and the church's social teaching.

C. What Actions Ought To Be Taken. (Handout's third column.)

Reference to the handout will provide a list of the action steps that are suggested. Essentially, there are two frameworks for the response; one is church-based, the other based in the international community.

1. *Church-based Action.* On the first level, the bishops call for justice within the institutional church itself. Just wages and benefits for those employed in the church are one aspect of this. Additionally, they call for a simplified lifestyle. Secondly, they emphasize education for justice. Its purpose would be multifold. On the one hand it would awaken the consciences of the affluent, and on the other, would conscientize the poor. The liturgy, the bishops claim, "can greatly serve education for justice." Thirdly, they call for collaboration among churches of different denominations and different economic status.

2. *International Action.* Paragraphs 63–71 contain a series of points advocated by the bishops. Most refer to support for the United Nations. Para. 67 calls for wider participation in decision making. Power is too concentrated, they suggest, for justice to prevail.

II. Document's Applicability

A. Group Comments

Refer first to the comments that the groups would have made during their reporting session. Then, mention again the bishops' statement that

Christians should be influenced in their lives by this teaching.

B. Methodology

Reflect on the methodology. Point out that the manner in which the synod approached and handled their subject can provide a model for a Social Ministry Committee to approach its efforts. See, Judge, Act provides a good manner for considering, studying and deciding upon involvements and actions.

The following diagram, which should be placed on newsprint or the blackboard, elaborates further on this model. It is the "pastoral circle" described in *Social Analysis,* by Joe Holland and Peter Henriot (Orbis Books, 1983). Thus depicted it represents a dynamic approach that continues beyond the "action." This same diagram is included in *Handout 3B.*

Analysis

Experience   Theological
                              Reflection

Action

Experience is the starting point. The perspective of the poor is central. *Analysis* is a study of the experience; it requires the gathering of facts, and going beyond isolated experiences which may not bear up under analytical scrutiny. *Reflection,* analogous to judging, brings the faith dimension into the process. Theology and prayer both have a role here. *Action* emerges from the reflection on the analysis.

4. Break: 10 min.

A member of the team should insure that refreshments are ready.

5. Leadership Functions: 25 min.

The remainder of this session relies heavily on input from the leaders. It is one of the few times that this method is employed so thoroughly. The

reason behind its use here is simply that this content possesses considerable importance for the group, but the constraints of time prohibit the use of structured exercises to make the points.

Two steps can help to make this less burdensome. First, apprising the group of the fact that lecture will predominate for the rest of the session will at least bring everyone's expectations into line. Secondly, lecturing in a dialogic manner, i.e., by engaging the group whenever possible through questions or personal references, can stimulate connections with the topic areas.

In this first area, Leadership Functions, key tasks that leaders must execute are discussed, and reference is made to a series of handouts.

Using *Briefing Paper 3B* as a guide, the leader will offer a lecture on this information. Opportunity will be given for questions.

BRIEFING PAPER 3B

Lecture on Leadership Functions

This section of Session III deals with the Tasks of Leadership, and it comments on some of the group process exercises that have already occurred earlier in the program. As with *Briefing Paper 3A,* what follows is a framework that includes pertinent notes for a lecture on this material. A variety of handouts are referred to as well.

Refer participants to *Handout 3C.* The front side lists the four Tasks of Leadership and two key leadership characteristics, the back contains a meeting preparation checklist.

This lecture highlights the subject of leadership and, through the handouts, provides some useful tools for effective group functioning. For some people who take part in the program, the following material may be redundant because of their own personal or professional experiences. However, this is not typically the case. Moreover, an understanding and implementation of these functions with the group are of critical importance for the group to thrive.

Engage the group as much as possible during this presentation. The heavy emphasis on lecture as a method is basically foreign to this program. However, in Session III it is used extensively. Consequently, it is important to draw people into the lectures by personalizing the material so that it does clearly pertain to them.

I. The Tasks of Leadership

By noting that, contrary to the opinion of some, leaders are made, not born, the facilitator sets the stage for an assertion that we all have leadership potential. Personality does not determine one's capacity to lead. On the contrary, a good leader is one who knows how to execute the tasks of leadership, and who does it. Through reference to the leadership qualities exercise in Session I the facilitator can remind the group that the qualities essential to leadership can be learned and refined.

In this introduction to the lecture, s/he indicates that in this section we will be examining the tasks that a leader must carry out. The examination will include the consideration of some materials that will be helpful to the leader in executing these tasks.

A. Planning

This first task requires the leader to look ahead, and take the steps, and make the arrangements necessary for the group's work to flow. An essential dimension of this involves meeting preparation. *Handout 3C* (back) provides a checklist that can be useful in doing this preparation. By reviewing this with the group, the nature of planning becomes evident. As most people have, at one time or another, had the experience of suffering through a totally unplanned meeting—a gathering with no agenda that started thirty-five minutes late in a room whose door was locked until ten minutes after it was supposed to start—it could be useful to relate just such an anecdote.

Planning is simply a job that has to be carried out if the group is to function effectively. It should be clear, moreover, that it relies far more on a person's initiative than on any inborn talent.

B. Running Meetings

Sometimes confused for leadership itself, the act of running meetings is just one of a leader's tasks. Like all of these leadership tasks, running meetings may come more naturally to some people than to others. Nonetheless, it is rare for someone

to be good at it if she or he has not learned the skill somewhere along the way.

Running a good meeting requires a chairperson who can move a group through a discussion to a decision. To do this the chairperson must allow the creativity of the group to flow. Stimulating but never dominating discussion, inviting participation of all members, especially quiet ones, and staying on schedule are all important tasks. The chairperson also must know the options that exist relative to making a decision. At times, sending the matter back to committee for further research or refinement or tabling it until more discussion time can be allocated are appropriate and good steps. At other times, they may be cop-outs. Experience helps the chairperson learn the options and the right time to employ them.

At various times during the course of this series, skills related to chairing meetings are identified. Awareness of them, and the willingness to practice them will help anyone become a better chairperson.

C. Administering

The group's leadership must also provide the administrative work needed to sustain it. At a minimum, this calls for record-keeping and for seeing that work commitments are completed. The former includes keeping and distributing minutes, and maintaining financial records. The latter makes the leaders responsible to keep in touch with group members, and to remind and/or assist them in carrying through with jobs for which they have taken responsibility.

D. Maintaining

This fourth essential task pertains to keeping the group together by tending to the morale of the group, and to the needs of each individual. Trust is perhaps the most important ingredient in the maintenance of a group, but it is by no means the only one.

For a person to make and keep a commitment to a group such as a Social Ministry Committee, he or she will have to be respected, included and affirmed. Each member must know she or he is more than a "warm body" that is filling out the rolls of the committee. Gatekeeping is an important function of the chairperson so that everyone will feel included in the decisions. It also serves to affirm each member whose opinion is solicited. Affirming, including, and respecting each member of a group will also help to establish the climate of trust needed to sustain the group.

Groups pass through various stages, and at times during the group's development, attentiveness to this maintenance task will be more important than at others. *Handout 3D,* "Stages of Group Development," offers an overview of these stages, and includes a column which describes the skills and tools needed to deal with the group during each stage. It is instructive to point out what these stages are, and what a leader needs to do to maintain the group at each stage.

II. Key Leadership Characteristics

A. Vision

A good leader will know where s/he is taking a group. To have such a vision for a parish social ministry organization, the leader needs to understand parish, social ministry, and organization. As with the leadership functions mentioned above, a person isn't born with this understanding, but acquires it through a variety of means. This process helps to provide all participants with some sense of vision by developing an understanding of social ministry, and some sense of how it can be brought to life in a parish. Together the group needs to be committed to developing vision through further study, dialogue, contact with groups from other parishes, and participation in workshops germane to social ministry in the parish.

B. Creativity

Creative people can take raw material and shape it into something others might never have considered possible. In the case of a social ministry organization, a creative leader might be able to take a group that is marginal to parish life, and move it right into its center. Creativity does not have to reside in the chairperson or other designated leaders, however, but is most effective when it, too, is a shared characteristic of the group. The leader's role may very well be simply to allow the potential creativity of the group to blossom.

III. Committee Organization: A Model of Operation

This part of the lecture will consist of reviewing two handouts.

Handout 3E provides the graphic for this model. By referring to it and reviewing the responsibilities of the task forces, the functional groups and the committee, participants see a committee model that is interdependent and dialogic. This model indicates that not everyone in the group needs to know all the details about every involvement. Small working groups take responsibility for various areas of the organization's work.

Task forces have the responsibility to work on the problems which the group chooses later in the process. They work as part of the larger organization to research, develop strategy and follow-up on the problems the committee has selected.

Functional groups meanwhile take responsibility for specific areas. The functions listed on the handout are ones which would fit under the mission of this organization, and if anyone will carry out these functions in the parish, the social ministry organization will be the likely group. For the most part, the agenda for the functional groups comes from outside the group. But the decision whether to participate in the related activity will belong to the group.

Handout 3F, meanwhile, provides some information about the internal organization of the group, with helpful information about its structure and operations.

6. Conflict Resolution: 25 min.

This is one aspect of group dynamics that is bound to be relevant and important for the group, both internally and in relation to other groups within the parish. Conflict has the potential for having strong negative consequences. The inability to face and/or resolve problems within the group can sap it of its energy and potential, while conflict with others in the parish can undermine its goal of catalyzing effective parish social ministry.

The information presented here will assist the group in identifying the nature of conflicts, the ways in which it is handled (or not handled), and in suggesting some approaches toward dealing effectively with it. Because of the lecture style, and the limited amount of time given to this, it can most helpfully be regarded as an introduction to the subject, albeit one that can help groups deal with this most important subject.

Briefing Paper 3C contains the lecture outline.

BRIEFING PAPER 3C: LECTURE ON CONFLICT RESOLUTION

The following lecture outline deals with the types, levels, and styles of conflict. It corresponds with *Handout 3G*.

I. Attitude Toward Conflict

At the outset several points should be made regarding conflict.

A. Conflict should be expected. Refer the group to *Handout 3D* and note that in Phase III of a group's development conflict should be anticipated.
B. Conflict itself is not a problem. The problem arises when it is not handled properly.
C. Conflict can be a group's best friend. If dealt with effectively, it can spark considerable creativity and be a key to sustained growth and success.

II. Types and Levels of Conflict:

Transition to this can be made by noting that in order for conflict to be a positive dimension of group life, it is necessary to understand it. Point out that *Handout 3G* outlines types and levels of conflict, and that the capacity to identify a conflict appropriately is a key step toward fruitful resolution of it.

A. Types

1. Intra-personal – within a person
2. Interpersonal – between interdependent persons
3. Intra-group – within a group
4. Intergroup – between groups

All of these types can influence a group, and they become progressively more difficult to re-

solve as they move from one to four. Type 4 might be manifest in disagreements between the committee and the parish council or the parish in general. Type 3 would obviously be within the committee itself.

B. Levels:

1. Facts or data: The parties involved have different information, and the conflict can be resolved by better communication.
2. Processes or methods: Parties agree on what has to be done but disagree on how to do it. More difficult to resolve than the first, it nonetheless is resolvable with the use of good techniques.
3. Goals or purpose: Disagreement here is over the mission of the group, and resolution requires negotiation and collaboration. This can be a source of difficulty for a Social Ministry Committee in relating to other parish groups that do not share their enthusiasm for the social mission of the church.
4. Values: This is the most difficult type of conflict to deal with, and typically requires third party mediation. Parties are coming from different places. (A related example of this type of conflict can be found in the varied reactions within the U.S. Catholic community to the various major pastoral letters which the bishops have written, starting with *The Challenge of Peace* in 1983.)

III. Styles of Behavior in Conflict Situations

The following conflict styles demonstrate the behavioral options available in facing a conflictual situation. Point out that no value judgment can be ascribed to them, but that different styles are appropriate in different contexts. Flexibility is key. (These styles are described on *Handout 3G*.)

1. *Avoiding* occurs when one or both parties withdraw from the conflict situation. They either do not acknowledge the existence of the conflict, or they refuse to deal with it.

It is appropriate to use when:

—the cost is greater than the benefits or rewards,

—priorities dictate that it is not wise to get side-tracked on less important issues,
—parties are overemotional and need a "cooling-off" period,
—parties agree to disagree.

2. *Accommodating* is a style through which the party emphasizes preserving the relationship by stressing common interests or areas of agreement and failing to confront areas of disagreement. This is often tantamount to giving in, and the use of this style can lead to being taken advantage of.

It is appropriate to use when:

—the relationship is more important than the issue,
—the other party's need seems greater,
—the balance of power is clearly in the other's favor.

3. *Compromising* takes place when the parties bargain so that each side gets part of what it wants and yields on part. Sometimes compromising is the best solution to a problem, but often parties compromise without really examining the alternatives, because "splitting the difference" seems to be the only solution.

It is appropriate to use when:

—the situation is deadlocked and you need to avoid a win/lose outcome,
—half a loaf is truly better than none at all,
—when shortness of time doesn't allow for further problem solving,
—when you want to preserve the relationship and further conflict on this issue would be too damaging.

4. *Competing* occurs when one side wins, forcing the other to acquiesce.

It is appropriate to use when:

—unpopular decisions have to be enforced,
—one believes strongly that s/he is right, and the outcome is very important,

—there is a crisis situation that requires quick action.

5. *Collaborating* involves agreeing to cooperate and attempt to find a solution that will meet the needs of both sides at a level sufficient to avoid feelings of losing. It is a time-consuming and difficult, but often rewarding style, based on the assumption that authentic dialogue and cooperation elicits the greatest rewards.

It is appropriate to use when:

—the issue holds real significance,
—the outcome has major implications for the future of the group, the organization or the relationship,
—the group can commit the time and energy to do creative problem solving, seeking the best solution from all possible alternatives,
—parties are committed to win/win solutions,
—all persons involved are committed to the outcome and its implementation.

IV. Tips for Dealing with Conflict

To close, the leader refers participants to *Handout 3H* which offers some specific hints on how to deal with conflict situations. Finally, the leader can reiterate that this lecture merely scratches the surface of conflict resolution, but it is a strong beginning.

7. Prioritizing Criteria: 15 min.

At this time, the criteria that the group will use in the evaluation of the social concerns the group identifies will be presented. The use of these criteria will commence after Session IV, and the prioritizing process will be the subject of Session V. Presentation and discussion of the criteria at this stage will foster a "cleaner" consideration of the list as individuals' pet projects that could affect the determination of criteria have not yet surfaced.

Handout 3I will provide the basis for this presentation and the discussion. Listed there are suggested criteria, which are divided into two categories—Must and Want. In each category there is space to add other criteria that the group may decide to include.

The Process

A. Review of the Criteria: 3 min.

Call the group's attention to *Handout 3I,* and offer a brief explanation of it. Ask them to read over the criteria, and invite questions from the group.

B. Discussion of the Criteria: 12 min.

Upon completion of the above step, invite participants to offer other suggested criteria that are not on the original list. There is also the possibility that the suggestion might be made to omit some of the criteria from the original list. Before that is done, discussion should be held and a clear consensus of the group should support it.

8. Preparation for Session IV: 5 min.

Handout 3J contains information regarding the work needed to be done prior to the next meeting.

The leader should emphasize the significance of the problem identification task that must be done in preparation for Session IV. By reviewing both *Handout 3K* and *Handout 3L* this point can be made.

SESSION III—HANDOUT 3A

Prayer Service

Theme: Worship, Sacraments and Work for Justice

Reflection Question: In what ways do I experience a link between the church's worship, sacraments and work for justice? How is my prayer life connected to work for justice?

Reading: Isaiah 58:2–8

Pause

Reading: Justice in the World, Paragraph 58.
   "The liturgy, which we preside over and which is the heart of the Church's life, can greatly serve education for justice . . . The liturgy of the word, catechesis, and the celebration of the sacraments have the power to help us to discover the teaching of the prophets, the Lord and the Apostles on the subject of justice."

Reading: John Paul II, *On Social Concern,* #48
   "All of us who take part in the Eucharist are called to discover, through this Sacrament, the profound meaning of our actions in the world in favour of development and peace, and to receive from it the strength to commit ourselves ever more generously following the example of Christ, who in this sacrament lays down his life for his friends. Our personal commitment, like Christ's and in union with his, will not be in vain but certainly fruitful."

Reflection Question: What is one way that I can connect my prayer life more intimately with my Christian social responsibility? What is one way my parish worship can reflect more fully the church's social mission?

Closing prayer: (All) Loving God, Creator of the air that we breathe and the food that we eat, help us to come to know you better through prayer and worship; help us to see your brilliance reflected in all peoples, and help us to carry out our mission to do justice. Amen.

Justice in the World

See—Justice and World Society

Crisis in Solidarity

- Paradox: division and antagonism in the midst of the promise of solidarity.
- Failure of trickle-down economics.
- Environmental peril.
- Unequal wealth distribution.

Right to Development

- Sinful obstacles in its way.
- Fear of new colonialism.
- Participation in economic and political areas is a right.

Voiceless Injustices

- Migrants, refugees.
- Religious persecution.
- Abortion, abandoned people.
- Restriction of individual's rights.

Judge—"The Gospel Message and the Church's Mission"

- Social *structures* can be sinful.

Salvation by God through Christ

- God is liberator.
- Jesus identified with the poor.
- Love of neighbor and justice are linked.
- Mission: liberation of people in present existence.

Mission of Church Hierarchy and Christians

- Love of God demands justice in the world.
- Giving witness.
- Defend dignity and rights of human person.
- Christians should be influenced by the gospel and social teaching

- Nonviolent action preferred.
- Church institution must deal justly with employees.
- Simple lifestyle.
- Education to justice.
- Rich church–poor church sharing.
- Work for justice ecumenically.
- 8 specific suggestions.
- Give flesh in local churches to this teaching.

The Pastoral Circle: A Means to Apply our Faith to Matters of Justice.

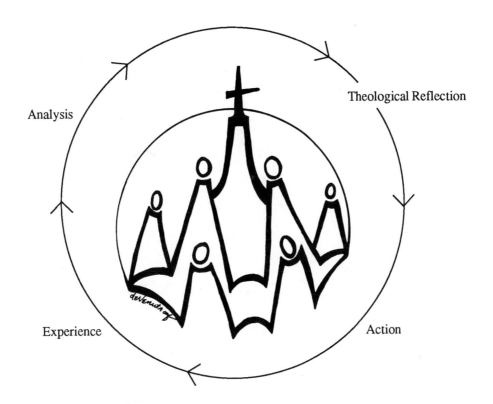

Experience: The starting point for the circle. For church people the experience of the poor holds special significance as we need to try to see through their eyes. It is through experience that we begin to *see*.

Analysis: In order to work for social change, the experiences must be subject to analysis so that the cause of problems can be accurately diagnosed. In this process, we *see* more clearly.

Theological Reflection: Once we have learned through experience and analysis, we must look to our faith to evaluate the situation. In this stage we *judge* the reality in light of principles of faith.

Action: Action comes after our judgment and manifests our commitment to put our faith into action. Here we *act*. Then the circle begins anew.

(Pastoral Circle adapted from *Social Analysis* by Peter Henriot and Joe Holland, Orbis Books, 1983)

SESSION III—HANDOUT 3C

Tasks of Leadership

Planning

Running Meetings

Administering

Maintaining

Two Key Leadership Characteristics

Vision

Creativity

Meeting Preparation Checklist

Preparation

_____ Meeting time and date:

_____ Place:

_____ Meeting objective(s):

_____ Agenda: (should include prayer, reporting, discussion, evaluation, planning, new business, announcements)

_____ Send notices to expected participants (include agenda)

_____ Identify and notify resource people needed

_____ Publicity

The Meeting

_____ Arrive early

_____ Set up facilities

_____ Start on time

_____ Introductions

_____ Review agenda and objectives (note time allocation)

_____ Agenda changes (if any)

_____ Establish ending time

_____ Proceed with agenda

_____ List of decisions and assignments:

_____ Time, date and place for next meeting:

Follow-up

_____ Compile minutes

_____ Disseminate minutes

Stages of Group Development

Stage 1: Getting Acquainted

Characteristics

- desire to get acquainted
- no conflict
- testing for comfort and acceptance
- cliques begin to form

Helpful Skills and Tools

- ice-breaker exercises
- structured exercises
- well-planned prayer
- name tags
- use of newsprint

Stage 2: Getting on with the Mission

Characteristics

- need to know group's purpose
- agenda needed
- group structure evolves
- broad participation
- members more secure

Helpful Skills and Tools

- written goals/objectives
- planning skills
- communication skills
- agendas and minutes
- prayer

Stage 3: Power Struggle

Characteristics

- competition
- conflict more likely
- cliques operating
- some dissatisfaction with group

Helpful Skills and Tools

- conflict resolution skills
- communication skills
- outside facilitator
- job descriptions
- prayer

Some Groups Never Move Beyond This Phase.

Stage 4: Reemergence of Cohesion

Characteristics

- positive attitude reigns
- team spirit builds
- leadership is shared
- openness to new ideas

Helpful Skills and Tools

- outside facilitators
- recruitment skills
- advanced training
- planning skills

Stage 5: Flying High

Characteristics

- high morale
- group loyalty

Helpful Skills and Tools

- use those developed in first four phases

Social Ministry Committee

A Model of Operation

Issue
Task Force

Functional
Group

Functional Group

Social
Ministry
Committee

Issue Task Force

Functional
Group

Issue
Task Force

Roles of Each Entity

Social Ministry Committee	*Issue Task Force*	*Functional Groups*
Overall Coordination	Takes on specific problems	Handles specific committee functions like:
Generation of Ideas	Researches	
Prioritizing Concerns	Defines action plans	• Legislative Network
Strategy Input	With SMC's help, implements plan	• Direct assistance to needy people
Allocation of Resources	Recruits workers	• Promotion of special collections (CHD, Rice Bowl)
Link with Parish/Council		

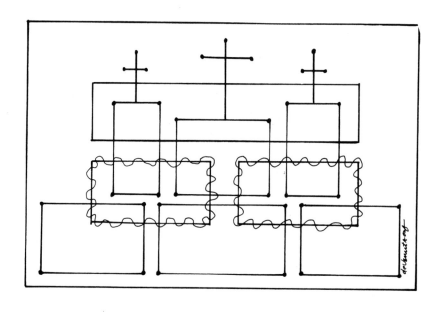

Group Structure and Operations

Officers

There is no set structure to adopt. The guideline a group needs to follow is simple: Have enough of a structure to ensure continued functioning, but not enough to become complex and bureaucratic.

Selection of temporary officers may be indicated for a newly formed group with permanent elections coming after people have had the chance to know each other better.

Regarding the process for selecting officers, it can be very helpful to establish a nominating committee which will approach people and invite them to "run" for a leadership position. It also serves a group well to have a defined term of office. It can entice prospective leaders to accept a nomination, knowing that the terms are set. It also protects the group from incompetent or ineffective leaders while allowing a greater number of people to share their talents. A one-year term that can be renewed once is a realistic period.

Continuity of leadership can also be built into the structure. A Social Ministry Committee would be well-advised to have at least a chairperson and a secretary.

Meetings

One of the leadership's prime functions is meeting planning. Agenda setting will have a tremendous influence on the directions that the group takes, and will help meetings be productive and interesting.

Regular meeting times and places assist people in remembering the group. The meeting place should be comfortable, and some form of refreshments should be available.

Membership Responsibilities

New members should be provided some orientation to the group. With that orientation they should be apprised of what specifically is expected of a member, including the term for which they are committing themselves, the types of involvements that are expected, and the amount of time on a weekly or monthly basis that members allocate for committee work.

Diagnosing Conflict

I. Types and Levels of Conflict
  A. Types
    1. Intra-personal—within a person
    2. Interpersonal—between interdependent people
    3. Intra-group—within a group
    4. Intergroup—between groups
  B. Levels: Resolution becomes more difficult at higher levels.
    1. *Facts or Data:* Parties have different information; better communication can solve the problem.
    2. *Processes and Methods:* Parties agree on what has to be done, but disagree on how to do it.
    3. *Goals or Purpose:* Disagreement pertains to mission of the group; resolution requires negotiation and collaboration.
    4. *Values:* Parties have differing value systems; most difficult to resolve, usually requires outside facilitator.
II. Styles of Dealing with Conflict
  The following styles demonstrate the options available when conflict arises. Different styles are appropriate at different times, and thus flexibility is key to successful management.

  A. *Avoiding* occurs when one or both parties withdraw from the conflict situation. They either do not acknowledge the existence of the conflict or they refuse to deal with it. (*Appropriate when:* the cost is greater than the benefits or rewards; parties are over-emotional and need a "cooling off" period.)
  B. *Accommodating* is a style in which the party emphasizes preserving the relationship by stressing common interests or areas of agreement and failing to confront areas of disagreement. It is tantamount to giving in, and its use can lead to being taken advantage of. (*Appropriate when:* the relationship is more important than the issue; the other party's need seems greater; the balance of power is in the other's favor.)
  C. *Compromising* takes place when the parties bargain so that each side receives part of what it wants, and yields on part. Sometimes compromising is the best solution; other times its use short-circuits the chance for more creative approaches. (*Appropriate when:* the situation is stalemated and you need to avoid a win/lose outcome; when half a loaf is better than none.
  D. *Competing* occurs when one side wins, forcing the other to acquiesce. (*Appropriate when:* unpopular decisions have to be enforced; one believes strongly that s/he is right and the outcome is very important; there is a crisis situation which requires quick action.)
  E. *Collaborating* involves agreeing to cooperate and attempt to find a solution that will meet the needs of both sides at a level sufficient to avoid feelings of losing. It is a time consuming and difficult, but often rewarding style, based on the assumption that authentic dialogue and cooperation elicits the greatest rewards. (*Appropriate when:* the issue is of great significance; the outcome has major implications for the future of the group, organization or the relationship; parties are committed to win/win solutions; time and energy is available.)

Practical Hints for Conflict Resolution

1. *Be understanding*
   In order to show concern for the person involved in the conflict one must display an understanding attitude. The deeper the conflict the greater the need for understanding.

2. *Be tentative*
   Clarify issues, identify the source of the conflict.

3. *Be honest about the conflict*
   Working through conflict is a way of reaching newer, deeper levels of relating. If one approaches it with this as a goal, the chance of resolution increases; if one approaches it to dump negative feelings, it is unlikely that any positive resolution will occur.

4. *Don't confront until you've earned the right*
   To earn the right to confront one must be open and have a decent relationship with the other. With no relational base, confrontation separates people further.

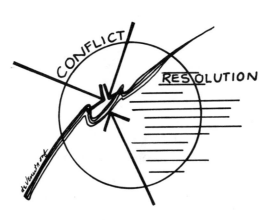

5. *Don't gang up on a person*
   It doesn't help a person to be confronted by many at once.

6. *Be definite*
   Make sure thoughts are expressed clearly—a vague notion of what troubles you is little help.

7. *Don't rely on nonverbal hints*
   Don't expect others to read your mind.

8. *Confront only if you want to grow closer*
   Confrontations enable people to deepen relationships, if the purpose is to do so. They can also be alarmingly destructive. If being constructive is the purpose, as it should be, it will influence the approach to raising and dealing with the issue.

9. *Don't get personal*
   Conflicts can heighten quickly if personal charges arise; focus instead on the issue needing resolution.

Prioritizing Criteria

The purpose of this handout is to provide you with some criteria to assist you in determining the initial priorities of your Social Ministry Committee. Some of these criteria will have a different degree of importance now than they might have after the committee is six months or a year old. For example, it often helps for a new committee to take on a project that can bring results in a few months' time, since taking on a concern upon which the committee can generate a quick, effective response is particularly important at the beginning of a committee's work.

What follows is a list of factors that should be considered when thinking about the group's initial involvements. You will use these to evaluate the problems that surfaced during next session's brainstorming. The first group represents criteria that *must* be met. The second are criteria that you would *want* to meet to some degree or another.

Must

—Pertinence to the church's social mission: Is the concern one which falls within the responsibility of the Social Ministry Committee?
—Feasibility: Can the committee really expect to do something effective about this concern?

Want

—Urgency: Is this a problem that is crying out for a response?
—Potential for Parish Involvement: Would this problem offer the opportunity for parishioners to act?
—Community-Building Potential: Would action on this matter tend to unify or divide the committee and parish?
—High Personal Interest: Am I willing to work on it?

SESSION III—HANDOUT 3J

SMC Organizing Process

Preparation for Session IV

"This Land is Home to Me"

Read "This Land is Home to Me" (Handout).
While reading, reflect on the following questions:
   —What do you understand to be the principal problems identified by the bishops of Appalachia?
   —What do they—the bishops—suggest that the church and the people do to respond to the problems?
   —What is your response to these readings? In what ways can they relate to your committee?

Problems

   Identify and list the problem that you would like your parish committee to consider for involvement. See *Handout 3K* for tips on how to identify problems.
   Fill out *Handout 3L,* and be prepared to make a brief presentation on your selected problem in Session IV.

SESSION III—HANDOUT 3K

Identifying Problems

Some possible steps—

I. Tapping Live Information Sources

Talk to people who might have special knowledge.
Possible sources of such information include:

—Pastor and other local clergy
—school officials
—law enforcement officials
—Department of Social Services Personnel
—participants in social services programs
—local business people
—senior citizens
—staff of Diocesan Social Ministry Offices
—local and county officeholders
—other

When talking to these people, tell them who you are, your parish affiliation and your interest in discovering what the problems are.

II. Tapping Written Sources

Some sources are easily accessible, others are less so; but both can provide helpful information. For example:

—local newspaper: read for purpose of uncovering needs/concerns/issues.
—census information: available in libraries, it can provide important background material on your community.
—Comparison with earlier census might point out changes that have occurred in the last decade.

III. Identify services available to people

Discovering what services are available can be a resource for the committee and also point out areas where services are lacking.
Discovering what is available in the following areas could be a start:

—senior citizens
—drug abuse/alcoholism
—single-parent families
—unemployment
—teenage pregnancy
—mental health
—other

Problem Identification

The problem which I would like our committee to consider addressing is _____
_____

My sources of information about this problem include

1. _____

2. _____

3. _____

Dealing with this problem would be important because _____
_____
_____

The problem is relevant to the social mission of the church for this (these) reason(s):_____
_____

Some possible actions we could take to respond to this problem include:

1. _____

2. _____

3. _____

SESSION IV

Introduction

By the fourth session, the social ministry organizing process has provided participants with a substantive orientation to the church's social mission and a solid overview of what is needed for a group mandated to carry out this mission to do so effectively. This session continues this process and adds more depth to the understanding of these two critical areas. It also begins the movement toward turning the process over to the group.

Two essential components make up Session IV. The first is the interrelated set of agenda items intended to show the explicit, practical link between faith and working for social change. The second component engages the group in identifying the problems which they want the group to address.

The precise media can vary but the essential point in the first component is that the church possesses very explicit teaching on justice, on what it is and on how we obtain it. The first item used to build this case is *This Land is Home to Me,* a pastoral letter which the bishops of Appalachia first issued in 1975, and reaffirmed in 1985. For the second item, we offer two approaches to convey success stories of social change. One suggestion is to use the Campaign for Human Development's 1988 video, "Building Partnerships." The alternative is to tell stories about successful efforts at bringing about social change. Lecture notes for such a presentation are provided. The final piece in this unit is a lecture on working for social change. It would be possible to use alternative media for the ninety minutes allocated for this, but the flow from theology to action should be carefully protected.

This Land is Home to Me incorporates the major principles of Catholic teaching on justice. In doing so, it suggests a pastoral response that has become normative for church efforts on behalf of justice. Specifically, "This Land" calls for citizen involvement in the shaping of economic, political and cultural structures that influence people's lives in all pervasive ways. "Building Partnerships" and the lecture apply that theology in showing precisely how people take charge of those structures. The lecture on social change dissects the process that the successful groups used.

Following this integrated unit comes the point where the group begins to really take over. Here participants identify the problems which they want the committee to take on as one of its first priorities. The process for selecting the top choices will make up the major part of Session V.

By now people are well-acquainted with the processes used, and generally have become comfortable with them.

SESSION IV—SUGGESTED USE OF TIME

10 min.	1.	Prayer
5 min.	2.	Recap
45 min.	3.	*This Land is Home to Me*
20 min.	4.	Making Change: Success Stories
10 min.	5.	Break
15 min.	6.	Working for Change
45 min.	7.	Identifying Social Concerns
5 min.	8.	Preparation for Session V

SESSION IV: LEADER'S PLAN

Objectives

A. Content

1. Consider the 1975 Appalachian Bishops' Pastoral Letter, *This Land is Home to Me.*
2. Examine the means of bringing about social change.
3. Identify problems the group may address.

B. Process

1. Continue group's experience of theological reflection.
2. Engage in process of identifying social problems that the committee might address.

Preparation

The facilities will need to be arranged as in earlier sessions. If the video is going to be used, it should be ready for showing.

Equipment needed for Session IV:

- newsprint and easel
- TV and VCR (optional)

Materials needed for session:

- packets of handouts
- video "Building Partnerships" (optional)
- *This Land is Home to Me*

Again, solid preparation by each leader is essential.

PROGRAM FOR SESSION IV

1. Prayer: 10–15 minutes

The theme of this session's prayer focuses on our responsibility to the poor. Through song, scripture and shared prayer, participants are invited to reflect on this obligation of our faith.

The prayer focus reinforces a theme that has prevailed both in the scripture study and in *Justice in the World*. What is outlined below is a very simple prayer that could be adapted with different music or supplemented with other components.

No handout is provided, but some provision should be made to make sure that people have access to the lyrics of the song. Music could be played on a tape recorder, or even better, could be led by a group member.

The Call to Prayer should invite the group to focus on our call to ministry with the poor, a ministry we take up out of faithfulness to a Creator who intends justice for all.

PRAYER THEME: OPTION FOR THE POOR

A. Call to Prayer

B. Song: "The Lord Hears the Cry of the Poor"

C. Reading: Luke 16:19–31. The story of the rich man and Lazarus.

D. Leader begins reflection on the gospel reading by noting how the rich man's sin was his failure to see Lazarus. That omission condemned him to eternal damnation. Invite the group to offer their own reflections on this passage, and how it calls them and the parish to responsibility.

E. Conclude with the Lord's Prayer.

2. Recap: 5 min.

The leader quickly reviews what has happened to date in the program, and reviews the agenda for this session. A note can be made that the identification of social problems in this session is the beginning of the committee's setting of its action agenda.

3. This Land is Home to Me: 45 min.

The leader directs the group to use the same methodology Session III utilized in its review of *Justice in the World*. It provides participants with the chance to talk with one another and reflect on this splendidly readable document.

Although it is more than a decade since this pastoral letter was issued, the reissuing of a tenth anniversary issue, signed again in 1985 by the bishops of the region, gives it ongoing relevance. Its unique, popular composition provides a welcome relief from the typically abstruse church documents. Also, because *This Land is Home to Me* addresses a very defined, local situation, it has greater specificity than Vatican documents.

As in Session III, then, the process begins with a small group discussion, continues with a large group convening, and concludes with a brief lecture.

The Process

A. Small Group Discussions: 15 min.

The leader begins by dividing the large group into small groups of 6–8 people. The small groups are then directed to gather in the various locations available and to spend the next fifteen minutes discussing the focus questions. Each group should appoint a recorder who will be responsible to report back to the larger group in the discussion that will follow.

During the discussion period, the leader might circulate unobtrusively among the groups in order to gain a sense of the conversations that are occurring.

B. Plenary Session: 15 min.

The large group reconvenes, and the leader starts by asking for small group reports from the recorders, inviting others to elaborate on the reports if they choose. Note on newsprint the key concepts that are articulated in each report.

The leader will also ask participants at this point if questions arose during their reading or discussion which have not yet been answered satisfactorily. Respond to them while maintaining consciousness of the time and the fact that some of them may be answered during the lecture that follows.

One should be aware that this particular document can elicit strong negative reactions from individuals who accurately perceive its negative characterization of capitalism. In such cases it is important to acknowledge that negativity. It should be pointed out that such a stand is a manifestation of the church acting as a prophet, calling attention to the economic system's failures to protect the dignity of the human person. It also needs to be noted that this critique does not imply sanctification of another system. Such a stand would take the church beyond the realm of its expertise. The bottom line is that the bishops of Appalachia are saying that we have a moral obligation to construct a more just system.

C. Lecture: 15 min. (Refer to Handout 4A)

Lecture. *Briefing Paper 4A* contains the necessary information for this. Points of emphasis can be adapted according to the discussion that has preceded it.

BRIEFING PAPER 4A

This outlines the lecture for the Appalachian bishops' 1975 pastoral letter, *This Land is Home*

to Me. As with previous outlines, the leader is advised to identify the major points articulated here, yet to adapt it into a form which is personally comfortable.

There is also some background information on the pastoral letter that may be helpful in developing anecdotes or in responding to questions.

BACKGROUND

Originally released in 1975, *This Land is Home to Me* joined twenty-six Roman Catholic bishops in a provocative plea for justice in Appalachia. It was the first time bishops in the United States had united in such a common cause, and it stands even today as perhaps the most sensitive and prophetic critique of our economic system's flaws.

Church workers in the region laid the groundwork for the pastoral letter, first by taking the initiative of having it drafted, and second by convincing the region's bishops to adopt it. The drafting process began with hours and hours of conversations with people of Appalachia who spoke of their hopes and dreams, as well as their suffering and oppression. These taped conversations provided much of the substance of the letter, and it is perhaps because of them that the document has such flavor of reality.

Episcopal support for the effort, however, was not a foregone conclusion. One priest involved in the project has said, in fact, that key support was generated from a most unlikely source—a corporate executive. The story goes that this executive made some derogatory remarks about working-class folk during a meeting with one of the region's bishops. The bishop in question was not, at the time, inclined to support the pastoral letter, but was apparently so provoked by these comments that he changed his mind. Unknown to the executive, the bishop's parents were working-class people. This turn of events, specifically the bishop's conversion, precipitated a rush to sign the document, as many heretofore reticent bishops added their names. The workings of the Spirit often can surprise us all.

The style of the pastoral letter, meanwhile, resulted from a deliberate attempt to avoid the typical ecclesiastical approach. Its free verse was published in newspaper form with drawings and graphics that related to the struggle of the mountain people, and this response to that struggle by the Catholic Church. Unlike most church documents, it was written to be read by the people.

The content, meanwhile, includes a rather radical analysis of the reality in Appalachia. Like many other church documents, *This Land is Home to Me* follows the see, judge, act format that *Justice in the World* introduced to program participants. Unlike many other documents, what they see is quite specific and provocative. Reportedly, some of the major corporations with interests in the region sought to hire a theologian to develop a rebuttal to it. As the story goes, they were unsuccessful in retaining anyone to do it. At any rate, *This Land is Home to Me* offers a highly readable application of Catholic social teaching to the contemporary Appalachian reality, and in doing so contributes to the theological bases for social concern.

LECTURE ON *THIS LAND IS HOME TO ME*

Introduction

In 1986, the U.S. bishops voted with near unanimity to approve *Economic Justice for All,* a controversial pastoral letter that applied Catholic social teaching to the reality in the United States. This pastoral letter was a watershed in the process of the U.S. Catholic Church's movement toward making work for justice a "constitutive dimension" of the preaching of the gospel in the United States.

EJA provides incisive reflection both on the nature of the responsibility of Christians living in a world that John Paul II has said is analogous to the story of the rich man and Lazarus, and on a series of issues that face the U.S. economy. In the process, EJA presented and applied a series of principles that are at the heart of Roman Catholic social teaching.

These principles also punctuate *This Land is Home to Me.* Appalachia, the impoverished mountain region in the eastern U.S., was the subject of this remarkable 1975 pastoral, which applied Catholic social teaching to a region that embodies characteristics of Third World countries.

I. The Perspective of the Appalachian Bishops

A. Biblical Parallel

In the opening verse of the pastoral letter, the bishops echo the words Yahweh spoke to Moses in the Book of Exodus. "We have listened to these cries and now we lend our own voice," they state.

B. Perspective of the Poor

Also in the introductory section, the bishops admit that they are looking at the Appalachian reality through the eyes of the poor. They admit that there are other vantage points from which to view Appalachia, but they argue that the views of the poor are those that they must consider by virtue of their faith in Jesus Christ.

II. Seeing, Judging, Acting

As with *Justice in the World,* the method used in this pastoral letter is see, judge, act. The first part of the letter details the reality of Appalachia, the second part judges it according to our faith, and the third part suggests actions we can take to create a more just and harmonious situation.

A. Seeing

What the bishops "see" in Appalachia is a social and economic system that exploits people for the purpose of profit, and in the process marginalizes the poor in such a manner that they are robbed of their right to self-determination.

A key symbol that they refer to is the idolatrous nature of profit. In the section entitled, "The Worship of an Idol," they make several strong statements indicting the system they are addressing. They write:

Without judging anyone
it has become clear to us
that the present economic order
does not care for its people.
In fact,
profit over people frequently are contradictory.
Profit over people is an idol.

B. Judging

In referring to the scripture and social teaching, the pastoral letter utilizes material that has been studied and discussed earlier in this process. God is a compassionate liberator who intervenes for those who suffer injustice. As a defender of justice, God freed the Israelites from oppression in Egypt, and ultimately sent a Redeemer whose Messiahship would be tied to the establishment of a reign of justice.

The mission of the church must be to carry on the work of this God, this Messiah.

C. Acting

In the pastoral's final section, "Facing the Future," the bishops do not offer specific solutions to the problems that they have brought to the surface. Instead, they offer principles which need to be the foundation of any just solution to the problems. These principles are: "closeness to the people, careful use of scientific resources, and a steeping in the presence of the Spirit."

Regarding the first, the bishops note that the fundamental goal in the justice struggle is "citizen control or community control. The people themselves must shape their own destiny." Regarding the third principle, the bishops declare,

We know that if this renewed presence
can mature into a convergence
with a thirst for justice,
a new Pentecost will truly be upon us.

More than anything else, the action that must take place is that of empowering people. Empowering the poor to take control of their destiny, and empowering the church community to take its stand with the poor and alongside the poor.

III. Principles in Catholic Social Teaching

"This Land" contains certain principles for action follow-up. It also incorporates the set of moral principles that grounds Catholic teaching on justice. These principles provide the basis for contemporary Catholic social teaching, and they can therefore be seen as the basis for other documents such as *Economic Justice for All* and *The Challenge of Peace.*

A. The Dignity of the Human Person

The human person is sacred. As such each one deserves reverence. The institutions of our society must respect this principle, and the Catholic perspective on justice will judge every institution accordingly. The bottom line: the economy must serve people, people are not made to serve the economy.

B. Human Dignity Can Only Be Realized in Community

"This Land's" action responses call for the building up of community as a means of responding to the overwhelming injustices that confront Appalachia. While that may be a realistic strategy, it also echoes this principle.

C. The Preferential Option for the Poor

In following Jesus, in heeding the Hebrew prophets, the Christian church can do no other than exercise this option for the poor. This principle echoes through "This Land" and it sets a distinct pastoral direction in a region like Appalachia. It also stands as a principle by which the U.S. Church will be increasingly challenged to abide.

IV. Pertinence of This Land is Home to Me

Beyond its analysis of Appalachia, *This Land is Home to Me* has a broader relevance to the church. What follows are several aspects of the pastoral that point to this.

A. Critical Negativity

This pastoral exemplifies a key function of the church in relation to society—prophetic critique. Like the prophets in Israel, and throughout history, this pastoral letter points out the failings of social structures, failings that are manifest by the injustice perpetrated by those structures. This function obviously does not endear the church to the powers that be any more than Jesus endeared himself to the moneychangers in the temple.

B. Focus of the Document

Unlike Vatican documents and pastoral letters of the U.S. bishops, this has a more definite, concrete focus. As such, it is decidedly more specific than documents like *Justice in the World.* It more directly serves to bring our scripture and social teaching to bear on the lives of churchpeople, and on issues and concerns that are particular to them. It thereby moves us closer to our own reality, and suggests a path that we too might take.

C. Idolatry/Social Sin

By emphasizing idolatry as they do, the Appalachian bishops give the term a renewed relevance, and applicability to our spiritual lives. Idols like profit over people get in the way of our worship of the true God, and by naming that particular idol, the bishops challenge an economic system whose animating motivation is profit.

The document also points out that social structures themselves are sinful. That is, idols such as that mentioned above turn people away from God, and thus are sinful. John Paul II elaborated on this in the 1987 encyclical, *On Social Concern,* in which he pointed to two particular "structures of sin," the quest for profit at any cost and the thirst for power.

Social sin refers to the embodiment of sin and injustice in society's structures, institutions, cultures and attitudes. People often are blinded to the manner in which these embodied sins lead to the suffering of others, and are therefore less free to change themselves and the structures.

Apartheid in South Africa may be one of the clearest examples of this kind of sinful situation. "This Land" also suggests others—a situation where profit is elevated over people, or a set of values that make material possessions the defining factor for human dignity.

This Land is Home to Me raises this subject in a most compelling way.

4. Making Change: Success Stories: 20 min.

This segment presents stories of organizations that have successfully brought about social change. The process leaders can either utilize the videotape "Building Partnerships: An Experience in Faith," or use the adaptable, optional lecture.

The Campaign for Human Development (CHD) produced "Building Partnerships" in 1988. The video features four groups which CHD has funded, and it places their work in a context of faith, drawing particularly on the pastoral letter, *Economic Justice for All.* It provides a concrete application of the theological principles and perspectives found in church teaching on justice, and illustrates case studies where people have been empowered to break the cycle of poverty. Every diocesan CHD office received a copy of the video, and it should be available from the diocesan office for loan. Copies of it, however, are available from CHD for $5.95 (Address: CHD, United States Catholic Conference, 3211 4th St. N.E., Washington, DC 20017-1194).

The optional lecture can serve in place of the video. It highlights four social change stories, and can easily be adapted to include local examples.

"Building Partnerships: An Experience in Faith"

The Process

A. Introduction: 5 min. or less.

In making a transition from the lecture on the document subtitled, "A Pastoral Letter on Powerlessness in Appalachia," the leader should note that one of the clear pastoral directions advocated to address the situation of powerlessness is the organizing of communities and groups. In this way, people who are unable to exercise control over their lives gain access to power. The video provides examples of this empowerment process, which could be considered to be the embodiment of this theology in the lives of the people and organizations depicted.

Introduce people to the video by noting that it will show examples of economic cooperatives run by worker-owners, and of community organizations that are dealing with local issues.

Also, describe BUILD (Baltimore United in Leadership Development). It is an interfaith, multiracial organization in Baltimore that has successfully fought redlining (a practice of banks and insurance companies that designates sections of a community ineligible for loans and policies), and has negotiated an agreement between BUILD and more than 100 corporations and the public school system to upgrade schools and provide job opportunities for graduates.

B. Show the video: 14 min.

OPTIONAL BRIEFING PAPER: MAKING CHANGE

Background

This optional briefing paper provides information which can be used to describe four successful efforts at making social change happen. The first example describes a campaign which affected Federal legislation, and the second is one which led to enactment of new state law. The third and fourth cases refer to community organizations that empowered neighborhood people to create change at the local level. The lecture can easily be altered so that local examples can be inserted in place of any one or more of these four case studies.

With the examples provided, the role which church people played is indicated.

MAKING CHANGE: SUCCESS STORIES

I. Transition from This Land is Home to Me.

Catholic social teaching, of which *Justice in the World* and *This Land is Home to Me* are representative, call for responses to injustice that would bring about social change. In our democratic society, we have the opportunity to effect change through the legislative process. We also have the right to organize and demand that human dignity and human rights be protected and preserved. The strategy of organizing powerless people to take control of their own destinies is one particular strategy that is suggested in *This Land is Home to Me.*

What follow are examples of successful social change efforts that have come about as a result of successful advocacy and through effective community organization.

II. Four Stories of Social Change

A. Bread for the World Campaign for WIC Funding Increases

The Women, Infants, Children (WIC) nutrition program has been among the most successful Federal poverty programs. It provides nutritional supplements for pregnant and lactating mothers, in-fants and small children. WIC has been proven effective in reducing fetal death and low birth weight, the two most common causes of infant mortality. Unfortunately, WIC has never received the funding adequate to serve all the women and children who are eligible. In 1989, only 51.3% of those who qualify could participate.

Bread for the World (BFW), an ecumenical organization that lobbies Congress on food and hunger issues, made increased funding for WIC its 1987 priority. BFW spearheaded a letter-writing campaign to U.S. Senators and Members of Congress that urged the Federal government to increase funding by $150 million in Fiscal Year 1988. This was part of a long-range strategy to get full funding for the program so that everyone who meets the income eligibility standard can participate in the program.

At a time when Congress was preoccupied with the Federal budget deficit, the campaign succeeded in securing an additional $73 million for WIC funding, thus providing benefits for 150,000 more women, infants and children than otherwise would have had access to the nutritional supplementation.

BFW accomplished this by mobilizing its local chapters and member congregations. Protestant and Catholic parishes throughout the United States participated in the letter-writing campaign.

B. Kentucky Welfare Reform Coalition Scores a Victory

In 1988, Kentucky's new governor faced a budget deficit estimated at $450 million. Despite the obvious difficulty that faced any group seeking to increase state spending, the Kentucky Welfare Reform Coalition (KWRC) dared to advocate a series of bills that would increase Aid to Families with Dependent Children (AFDC) benefit levels while reforming the state's welfare programs to remove the work disincentives that plagued the system and kept people from freeing themselves from dependency upon it.

KWRC's membership includes AFDC clients, community action groups, and church representatives. The coalition lobbied the state legislature diligently, had members testify before legislative committees, generated countless letters of support, and drew heavily on a study done by the state's Legislative Research Commission. The study showed that Kentucky's AFDC benefits ranked the state 44th in the nation as they provided clients with only 25% of the funds needed to reach the Federal poverty line.

In the process of their 1988 campaign, KWRC won the support of the governor and of key leaders in the legislature for a comprehensive reform package that increased benefits and also provided incentives for clients to work. When the state's General Assembly adjourned, KWRC had scored a victory that only the most optimistic would have conceived possible before the Assembly convened. The Kentucky legislature had voted unanimously for the largest benefits increase in history, and had provided incentive for people to seek work without worrying that they would immediately lose their medical benefits when they began to earn a small income.

Church groups, including the Kentucky Council of Churches and the Catholic Conference of Kentucky, supported by church members throughout the state, were instrumental in aiding KWRC's efforts. Church members wrote letters, attended rallies, and urged the legislators to endorse the KWRC-supported bills.

C. COPS Provides a Powerful Voice

The Community Organizing Project of San Antonio (COPS) is an organization of 90,000 families that has been built from a base of religious congregations in the Texas city. A recipient of grants from the American bishops' Campaign for Human Development, it has provided its predominantly low-income and Hispanic membership with a powerful voice in civic affairs.

COPS has empowered individuals who had no say in the multitude of decisions that affected their lives to become lively participants in shaping programs and policies that have transformed the city and, most importantly, their neighborhoods. As with any successful community organization, it has made possible the development of leaders from within the community, leaders who brought the organization to victory after victory.

COPS helped resolve neighborhood drainage problems, spearheaded a successful voter registra-

tion drive, and helped gain over $500 million in improvements in the city's neighborhoods.

Churches provide the base of support and membership for the organization, as it is the church members themselves who were victimized by the problems it addresses and who became the leaders of the efforts to overcome them.

D. People for Community Recovery Cleans Up[1]

People for Community Recovery (PCR) provides an example of a community group that has brought change to a small section of a big city. The changes have made a big difference, however, to the people who live in Altgeld Gardens, a housing project on Chicago's southeast side.

Founded in 1982 when ten people gathered in a Methodist Church, PCR met with its first success when, after two years of pressure, it got the Chicago Housing Authority to agree to remove the asbestos from Altgeld Gardens' homes. The group had been provoked to this action by the alarming notice that their area had the highest cancer concentration in the city.

Subsequent accomplishments have included getting Chicago to provide city water and sewage hookup to a neighboring project, successfully advocating for the establishment of a medical clinic in the neighborhood (and thus making it unnecessary for those needing medical treatment to travel 90 minutes on public transportation to receive it), and convincing a landfill operator to put aside $25 million in a trust fund for the community.

PRC meets in Chicago's Our Lady of the Gardens Church.

III. Closing

These four examples point to successful social change efforts. Some were very local in scope, one impacted the deliberations of Congress. In each case, churches and churchpeople play an indispensable role. And in every case, success occurred because of the effective use of power.

1. See "Salt of the Earth: Hazel Johnson" in *Salt,* Vol. 8, No. 7, July/August, 1988.

5. *Break: 10 min.*

6. *Working for Change: 15 minutes.*

The leader here makes a brief presentation on the means that must be used to bring about social change. It refers to both the film and the pastoral letter, using them for the theological and tactical background. The material for this can be found in *Briefing Paper 4B. Handout 4B* outlines the lecture.

BRIEFING PAPER 4B

This lecture will highlight the information drawn from *Empowerment* by Harry Fagan. (Paulist Press, 1979.) Reference back to either the video or the lecture will make concrete the theoretical principles. The facilitator can also make use of local examples which s/he may be familiar with that are also examples of the application of these ideas.

The fundamental point of the lecture reiterates the message of the previous section, and the experience of any successful social change effort. In order to bring about change, a group must have power, and in order to have power a group needs knowledge and people.

LECTURE ON KEYS TO SOCIAL CHANGE

I. Keys to Social Change: Knowledge and Constituency = Power

A. Knowledge

Obviously nothing will change unless we can identify what needs to change, and how it needs to change in order to solve our problem. Research is therefore essential so that we can answer the companion questions: Who is doing What to Whom? Why? When? Where?

Effective change agents know what needs to happen for a problem to be overcome, and they also know who has the power to bring about the desired action. They need to know why the problem exists and whose interests are served by its continuation.

Successful organizations such as those noted in the video (and lecture) found the answers to these questions.

B. People

In order to put the knowledge to use for the purpose of social change it is necessary for a sufficient number of people to show their support. The same was true for the community organizations in the video (and lecture). Without the combination of the two, the power needed to challenge the status quo doesn't exist.

C. Power

Harry Fagan indicates that this word has a lot of baggage, and folks don't like to associate it with church. Simply stated, however, power is nothing more than the ability to act. Reviewing the theology we have studied indicates that people have the right to determine their own futures. They have the right to be out from under the subjugation of another. Oppression by its very nature denies people the power to control their own lives and violates their human dignity.

The exercise of power on behalf of justice, therefore, is an important element of our lives as Christians.

II. Effective Use of Power

Fagan suggests that the effective use of power depends upon the group accurately defining a problem, grabbing onto the problem by identifying a specific issue related to it, and charting a course of action that can effectively address the issue. There is a logical progression to these three steps—from problem to issue to action, and whether a parish group is involved in a social change initiative or in a direct service project this schema is useful.

Moving from problem to issue to action permits us both to think globally and act locally. While problems may be immense, issues allow us to get a hold of them in order to take effective action in the parish.

For example, homelessness can depress anyone and any group that lets the whole problem weigh heavily on their shoulders. But a parish that assists a non-profit housing corporation and furnishes an apartment for a low-income family takes effective action on the problem.

Meanwhile, the dreadful economic plight of many single-parent families should provoke shame for our society's callousness to the condition of these "widows and orphans" of our day. Being part of a local coalition or letter-writing network working for effective welfare reform, however, can channel our energies toward positive and fruitful ends. In either case, the problem needs to be known, the issue identified and an action taken if we are to use the power at our disposal.

III. Pitfalls

Things can get in the way of using power effectively. Three tendencies that Fagan illustrates are paralysis by analysis, being an idealistic liberal, and playing the do-gooder game.

A. Paralysis by Analysis: We can be stymied by trying to gather too much information and being overwhelmed by its complexity. Sooner or later, we have to take our stand and move beyond the mind games that can trap us in inaction.

B. The Idealistic Liberal: Fagan regards this person as least willing to accept the problem-issue-action framework. S/he leaps to fantastic ideological heights quickly and with little practical sense.

C. The Do-Gooder Game: This exercise engages people in devising impossible goals so as to relieve any possible guilt over not accomplishing anything. Instead of accountability which requires discipline and measurable efforts, the do-gooder game takes people into the netherworld of unachievable albeit noble goals.

7. Identifying Social Concerns: 45 minutes

If more than one parish is participating in the training program, the group will have to be split according to parish lines. The technique that will be used has been introduced to the people through the assignment for the session. Each person has been asked to identify one social problem that they would like the group to address. These problems will be presented during this session.

A window is also left open for some brainstorming on problems. Unfortunately, despite the importuning of leaders, some people will be winging it when the identification of problems occurs. The leader might have to permit this in order to give everyone the opportunity to be involved in this most important step.

The Process

A. Description of the Process: 5 min.

The leader will begin by describing the objectives of this section, noting the purpose of identifying the group's concerns, and by indicating the method that will be used. That method is as follows:

1. Each individual will be asked to identify and elaborate upon the problem he/she wants the group to address, being given 3–5 minutes for the presentation. Time should be allocated according to the number of people in the group, and the amount of time for this step.

2. Problems will be listed on newsprint, and other group members will ask any clarification questions they might have. The leader will have to limit the questions to ones of this type. This is not the time for discussing the merits or nature of the problem. Participants also write the problems listed on *Handout 4C*.

Process will continue until each person has presented his/her problem.

B. Process Implemented: 35 min.

The leader will implement the process as described above.

C. Clarification: 5 min.

After the presentations are completed, the leader will offer one final opportunity for clarification of items that are unclear to some. The person who identified the problem should be given the chance to clarify it.

D. Next Step: 1 min.

The leader points out that the group should have copied the list from the newsprint. The criteria adopted earlier in the program will be used to evaluate the problems. For next week, *Handout* *4E* and *Handout 4F* will be used. In preparation for Session V, the group will be asked to evaluate the problems according to the *Must* and *Want* criteria.

8. *Preparation for Session V: 5 min.*

Review *Handout 4D.*
Handouts 4E and *4F* should be pointed out, and a brief explanation of them should be given.

This Land is Home to Me

Outline for Lecture

I. The Perspective of the Appalachian Bishops
   A. Biblical Parallel

   B. Perspective of the Poor

II. Seeing, Judging, Acting
   A. What the bishops see

   B. How the bishops judge the reality

   C. What actions the bishops recommend

III. Principles of Catholic Social Teaching
   A. Dignity of the Human Person

   B. Human Dignity: Realized only in Community

   C. Preferential Option for the Poor

IV. Pertinence of *This Land is Home to Me*
   A. Critical Negativity: Prophetic Stance

   B. Focus of the Pastoral Letter

   C. Idolatry and Social Sin

Working for Change*

Lecture Outline

I. Keys to Social Change: Knowledge + Constituency = Power
  A. Knowledge
  B. Constituency
  C. Power: The ability to act

II. Effective Use of Power
  A. Identifying the Problem
  B. Choosing an Issue
  C. Developing a Strategy for Action

III. Pitfalls
  A. Paralysis by Analysis
  B. The Idealistic Liberal
  C. The Do-Gooder Game

* Material for this lecture is drawn from *Empowerment* by Harry Fagan (Paulist Press, 1979.)

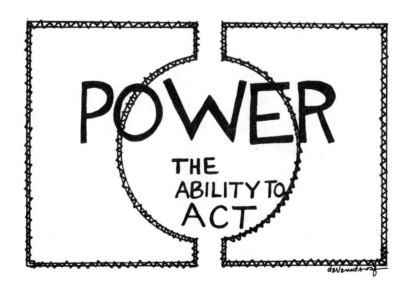

SESSION IV—HANDOUT 4C

Problems Identified

List below the problems that your group is identifying during the related part of Session IV. Describe them fully enough so that you will be able to remember key elements of the problem.

1. _____

_____

2. _____

_____

3. _____

_____

4. _____

_____

5. _____

_____

6. _____

_____

7. _____

_____

8. _____

_____

9. _____

_____

SESSION IV—HANDOUT 4D

Preparation for Session V

First, evaluate the problems listed by the group according to the "Must" criteria. Use *Handout 4E*.

Second, evaluate the problems according to the "Want" criteria. Use *Handout 4F*.

Third, if there are one or more problems that you are particularly interested in, but would like more information about, use the time between sessions four and five to do additional research. This step is especially important if you want to help persuade the group to adopt a specific problem as a priority.

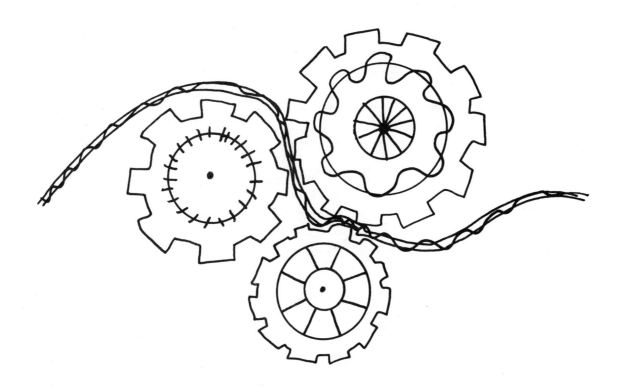

SESSION IV—HANDOUT 4E

"Must" Criteria Screening

In Session II the group agreed to a set of criteria that must be met by the problem it will address. The grid below provides room to list the problems identified in Session IV in the vertical column, and it already lists the "must" criteria in the horizontal column (with space left for other criteria that may have been added).

Evaluate each problem by marking in the appropriate column a "yes" if the problem satisfies the criterion, and a "no" if it doesn't.

	Problem	*Social Mission*	*Feasibility*	*Other*
1.				
2.				
3.				
4.				
5.				
6.				
7.				
8.				

SESSION IV—HANDOUT 4F

"Want" Criteria Screening

The "Want" criteria include elements which the group wants to characterize the problems it prioritizes. Unlike the "must" criteria, these criteria can be measured by degree. So in place of the "yes" or "no" answers on the previous screening, grade each problem using the following scale:

$$3 = high \qquad 2 = medium \qquad 1 = low$$

Again the problems can be listed in the vertical column, and the criteria are in the horizontal column. Evaluate each problem according to all the criteria.

Problem	Urgency	Involvement Potential	Community Potential	Personal Interest
1. ___				
2. ___				
3. ___				
4. ___				
5. ___				
6. ___				
7. ___				
8. ___				

SESSION V

Introduction

Almost all of Session V is committed to the process of prioritizing the problems that the group has identified. It requires deftness and discipline on the part of the leader, and it is, over the long term, the most consequential of the six sessions.

The leader's notes offer a prescribed process for the group to select its priorities. They draw upon the criteria introduced in Session III, and employ a series of techniques to help the group reach a decision.

The steps indicated work. They provide a disciplined approach for the group's decisions on priorities. Taking a good, hard look at possibilities, and using agreed-upon criteria in the selection are the two key points. The leader should feel free, therefore, to modify this process according to one's own style and to the situation of the group.

Discipleship is the theme for this session's prayer. Such a theme is appropriate for a group that is nearing commitment on how it will animate the church's social mission in its parish.

The one other element in Session V is entitled "Ways of Responding." This input section points out that a wide variety of responses are available to redress any problem. In addition, it demonstrates that there are different approaches to each problem, and recalls the essential lesson in Session I regarding the two sides of social ministry.

SESSION V—SUGGESTED USE OF TIME

15 min.	1.	Prayer
5 min.	2.	Recap
65 min.	3.	Prioritizing
10 min.	4.	Break
45 min.	5.	Prioritizing (cont.)
10 min.	6.	Ways of Responding
5 min.	7.	Preparation for Session VI

SESSION V: LEADER'S PLAN

I. Objectives

A. Content

1. Prioritize concerns that the group will address.
2. Examine the types of action that can be taken.

B. Process

1. Group will go through prioritizing process.
2. Presentation on Frameworks for Action
3. Prayer/Reflection

II. Preparation

As in previous sessions, facilities will be arranged appropriately. Again a separate room may be needed for group work.

Equipment needed for fifth session:

- newsprint and easel
- tape player

Materials needed:

- tape player for prayer (optional)
- handouts for session V

Finally, each leader will prepare respective sections.

PROGRAM FOR SESSION V

1. Prayer: 15 min.

The theme of this prayer service is Discipleship. It will be developed by a brief introduction, a

99

song, two short gospel readings, reflections on the readings, a second song, and a closing prayer. As with other prayer services, adaptation according to the preference of participants is encouraged.

A. Introduction

The leader identifies the theme, and the process that will be used for the prayer service. In introducing the theme, it would be appropriate to indicate that Jesus' disciples—at least according to the Gospel of Mark—neither quite understood Jesus when he told them what they must do as his followers, nor were they able to pass their first tests. Peter's denials, their falling asleep in the garden, and their fleeing when Jesus was arrested are three examples of their failure. Being a disciple, Mark seems to say, requires us to go beyond our own preconceptions of what Jesus asks, and to listen still again to what he is saying. In this prayer today may each person reflect anew on her or his call to follow Jesus.

B. The Prayer Service

1. Opening Song: "Here I Am, Lord"
   St. Louis Jesuits

2. Readings
   a. Mark 8:31–38
      Pause
      Brief reflection by the leader.
   b. Mark 10:42–45
      Pause
      Reflection by the leader/group.

3. Song: "Be Not Afraid"
   St. Louis Jesuits

4. Closing Prayer
   Lord, we go forward in our world
   not always certain we understand your
      will,
   and fearful when we think we do.

   Be with us, Jesus, as we struggle
   to know your will for us
   and to follow in your way.

   We pray for this wisdom and strength
   in the name of Jesus Christ.
   Amen.

2. Recap and Agenda Review: 5 min.

The principal point that the leader makes at this time is that this session culminates the process. Simulation exercises are over, theological bases have been constructed, identification of problems completed. Now the group will determine its action agenda. In so doing it will take the first significant action that will hopefully incorporate much of the group's experience from the program's first four sessions.

It would be helpful to note here that the process that will be used in this session aims to facilitate a collaborative decision. It is not a perfect model for consensus decision making, but it does attempt to approximate consensus. A definite goal is for all members to be able to live with the group's choices, and for each person to have one problem which s/he will want to address.

3. Prioritizing: 65 min.

There are a series of steps in this process. Some are fairly mechanical, others require an artful touch from the leader. The latter, moreover, are the ones critical to the group's decision making. The explanation of the steps can only be a guide to the leader who must be ready and able to shift direction while moving the group to its decision.

Remembering several basic elements will assist the leader in her/his task, including:

—the group's choosing to focus on a predetermined number of problems;
—the criteria that the group has agreed to use in making its decision;
—that elimination of items from the list only means they will not be the initial priorities of the group. They may very well become the basis for future action.

Each of these can assist the leader in keeping the group focused on its task.

A. Clarification: 10 min.

Prior to starting the prioritizing process, the group can request clarification on any of the problems that were identified at the previous session. The purpose now is not to debate or discuss the problems, but simply to explain those that may be unclear.

B. Number: 10 min.

The second step before prioritizing involves the group's decision as to how many problems they will address. Depending upon the group's size, there may be between ten and twenty items on the list. At this point, the group should decide how many of those it will adopt as priorities.

Frequently, groups resist taking this step. They may rightly argue that each problem requires a variable commitment, and they cannot assess this adequately. Be that as it may, the leader must encourage the group to take this step in order for the session's process to proceed. It is essential for the group to set this goal before the prioritizing can begin. If necessary, the leader can urge the group to choose a number that may be changed later if the group consents.

A good rule to observe in this process is that the group choose no more than one problem for every five people on the committee. A ten or twelve person committee would be safe to choose two, but may be pushing it to try three. A fifteen member committee, however, may be well able to handle three problems.

C. "Must Criteria" Screening: 10 min.

Each person was asked to prepare for this session by reviewing the problems identified last time according to the "must criteria." At this point, the facilitator should ask if there are any items on the list which the consensus holds should be eliminated because they fail to meet these fundamental criteria.

It frequently occurs that none are removed from the list during this step. That happens because most groups only identify problems relevant to the church's social mission, and effective action can be taken on almost any problem, as long as an appropriate issue is defined. It does happen, however, that "off the wall" ideas get listed, and that good ideas whose parameters fall outside the bounds of this committee find their way onto the agenda. Concern for education in the parish seems to be one of the latter that predictably arises. This

is the time to remove them if they are on the list, and if consensus can be established that they fail to meet the established criteria.

The leader has to be careful to keep the focus on the "must criteria," as there is a tendency to broaden the scope of the discussion immediately.

D. "Want Criteria" Reassessment: 5 min.

The facilitator now asks the participants to re-evaluate the ideas on the list according to the "want criteria." *Handout 4F* provides the grid for this step, and the group can now review their preparation of this handout.

In a variation from the "must criteria," the group will give numerical grades for each problem under the respective criteria. Using numbers one, two and three to indicate low, medium and high priority, respectively, participants will grade each problem according to the four "want criteria."

In starting the group on this task, it is helpful to give one concrete example. If homelessness may be a problem the group has identified, the leader can, hypothetically, rank it as a three for urgency (If it is a critical local problem), a two for potential for parish involvement (If you think a fair number of people would become involved), a one for community-building potential (If you may want to use the old convent as a shelter and you suspect some parishioners might object), and a two for personal interest (If you could get interested in it). Each problem should be evaluated in this way by each person.

The leader should also note that these numbers are intended to assist the group in discussion and decision making. They will not, however, be precisely calculated to determine the group's selection.

E. Open Discussion: 25–30 min.

Participants will here engage in discussion of the concerns that they would most like the group to adopt. The criteria should provide the framework for this discussion, but the facilitator should not be too insistent on this point. A key role for the facilitator here is gatekeeping. In this case, gatekeeping means two things. First, it implies insuring that everyone has the opportunity to contribute. Second, it means that the group does not mire the discussion on one or two topics, but that reference to the entire list occurs.

During this opening discussion, people should either promote their favorites or suggest problems they think should be removed from the list. Importantly, they will have more time to continue their discussion during the break, and after it.

4. Break: 10 min.

5. Prioritizing (cont.): 45 min.

A. Straw Vote: 10 min.

As a means of gaining a sense of the group's opinion, the leader begins the post-break session by inviting the group to vote on their favorites. This is not going to determine the final selection, and that point should be noted. Instead, it is intended to shorten the list, and further focus the group.

The straw vote may demonstrate the clear favorites of the group. The facilitator must be wary, however, of jumping to conclusions, and must always test for consensus before taking steps such as eliminating items from the list. The steps that follow should indicate a way to deal with this process so that it can be as useful as possible.

—*First,* ask individuals to choose the three (or five) items on the list that they most want the group to address. (5 min.)
—*Second,* tally the results on newsprint. An easy way to do this is to list numbers that correspond to each problem on newsprint before beginning, and when tallying put slash marks next to the numbers named as they identify their preferences. Add up the number of votes that each received.
—*Third,* test for group consensus to eliminate those with no votes. It is unlikely that anyone will object.
—*Fourth,* assess the items that received only one vote. Let the group decide if these, too, should be erased. Remind the group that the goal is to end this session with the agreed upon number of priorities.

—*Fifth,* evaluate the top vote-getters. Test to see if there may already be a clear consensus on one or two items.

B. Continued Discussion: 15 min.

As with the earlier open discussion, the leader serves as a gatekeeper, but this time begins to attempt to hasten the decision. Keeping the group focused on its task is very important, and helping it make the hard decisions is the key task. Most importantly the leader must strive not to lose anyone by moving too precipitously to a decision.

C. Top Priorities Indicated: 20 min.

If the obvious choices have not yet emerged, or if only one of the two or three has surfaced, further individual choices should be requested. This time the question should be: On what one (or two) concern(s) are you willing to work? (If the group is asked to choose more than one item, weigh the responses accordingly when tallying such as by giving two votes to the first choice and one to the second.)

Tally the results of this. From here the facilitator must use his or her wits to finalize the outcome. It should be narrowed considerably at this point. It is possible to use time from Session VI for further prioritizing, but that should be the last resort.

6. Social Ministry—Ways of Responding: 10 min.

This brief section intends to offer participants a panorama of the types of action they can initiate. *Handout 5A* offers a way of seeing the options available to the group. The handout includes a schema that offers guidance in the development of an action plan. It suggests a full range of options available to a group as it moves from the articulation of problems into a response to them.

This intends to expand the group's frame of reference with respect to what they might do. Instead of responding to a problem with the first idea that comes to mind, this can assist participants to deal more systematically with the options available to them.

The Process

Review of Handout 5A

The leader reads over the handout with the group. S/he makes the distinction between the three approaches of education, service and action; they can be related to Session I and the discussion of the nature of Social Ministry Committee work. Then, the leader refers to the different levels. Besides an increase in the potential for controversy in higher level activities, there also typically is an increase in the complexity of the task. On the positive side, however, the higher profile activities will be more likely to put the committee on the parish map, and are likely to have more public implications.

This chart does make an important point that a committee can be involved in working for social change at a variety of levels. It demystifies, to a certain extent, the aura that sometimes surrounds social action, and gets a handle on how a parish committee can become involved in such efforts without becoming too controversial or too over-committed.

7. Preparation for Session VI: 5 min.

Handout 5B contains the assignment for Session VI. It depends upon the results of Session V to determine which of the two alternative assignments will be given.

If the prioritizing process is completed in Session V, the group is asked to use *Handout 5C* to consider how to address one of the group's chosen problems.

SESSION V—HANDOUT 5A

Social Ministry: Ways of Responding

Any social problem can provoke a very wide range of responses. Choosing what to do requires an accurate understanding of the problem and a sound assessment of the resources which can be garnered for the effort. Creative responses also are more likely to be generated by groups that have a view of a full range of options.

The grid that follows suggests the range of options available when addressing the problem of hunger. The three approaches to the problem are education, service and action. The three levels noted on the grid point to the various levels at which a group can choose to respond, with the higher level connoting a more thorough and complex involvement.

Using the same grid for any problem can help identify the various responses that can be mounted to address it. Too often the first idea raised becomes the direction the group follows. While that isn't necessarily bad in all cases, it does signal a failure to review the options and in some cases, to be sure, it will mean the group's potential to have an impact will not be reached.

The grid can provoke a most creative brainstorming session and thereby generate an exciting list of potential action steps.

RESPONSES TO THE PROBLEM OF HUNGER

Approaches / Levels	Education	Service	Action
Low	Study problem of world hunger.	Organize a food drive in the parish.	Join "Bread for the World."
Medium	Offer a seminar on hunger's resurgence in the U.S.	Set up a local food pantry.	Lobby Federal lawmakers to provide adequate funding for food programs.
High	Research local food and nutritional needs.	Help establish a soup kitchen in a place where it will serve the most people.	Raise funds to support a self-help food project.

SESSION V—HANDOUT 5B

Social Ministry Committee Training
Preparation for Session VI

Prioritizing

If the group has not completed the prioritizing process by the conclusion of Session V, the task for Session VI calls for individuals to do some further research on problems still in contention. That information will provide the basis for discussion in the last session when the choices are finalized.

Note: Each member should be involved in this. If there are more people than problems to research, individuals should work in small groups. Research should include input from a variety of sources: experts, service providers, victims and change agents all have differing and valuable perspectives on a given problem.

Action Proposal

If the priorities are set, group members should denote which problem they will choose to work on. To prepare for the sixth session each person should refer to their respective choice and

1. Fill in the blank grid on *Handout 5C* with the possible responses to the problem for each approach and each level;
2. Choose from the grid the response which would be most appropriate for the group to make.

Approaches / Levels	Education	Service	Action
Low			
Medium			
High			

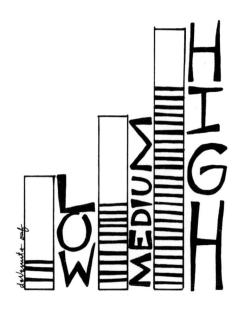

SESSION VI

Introduction

Just as Session I cracked open the four areas of theology, group process, social ministry skills, and spirituality, Session VI brings closure to the treatment of them in this six-session process. Hopefully, the group will know that they will have to continue to look for opportunities to grow in each of these areas as they carry out their ministry in the parish.

Session VI opens with a brief prayer that centers folks on discipleship and the Reign of God. The prayer will continue, developing this theme further, later in the session.

More decisions on the group's priorities will be made in the first major section on this session's agenda. In Session III, we introduced an organizational model for the group. The issue task forces handle the problems chosen in Session V. The functional groups take on functions of the organization that, in a certain sense, are already defined, and for which the group makes the decision whether to plug into them or not. Choosing which functions they will assume takes place at this time.

After completing this first task, the group breaks into issue task forces. These small groups will begin to select action steps which the organization will take to respond to the respective problems. The dynamics of this agenda item exemplify a dialogic committee process.

The remainder of the agenda focuses on bringing the process to a close. Summary descriptions of the organization's relationships to other groups, inside and outside the parish, and of the role of theology and spirituality in the group's life conclude the content section of the process. Evaluation of the six sessions ends the process.

SESSION VI—SUGGESTED USE OF TIME

5 min.	1.	Prayer
5 min.	2.	Recap
20 min.	3.	Components of Committee
45 min.	4.	Small Group Meetings
10 min.	5.	Break
10 min.	6.	SMC Perspectives
15 min.	7.	Theology Summary
30 min.	8.	Spirituality and the SMC
10 min.	9.	Evaluation
10 min.	10.	Closing

SESSION VI: LEADER'S PLAN

I. Objectives

A. Content

1. Provide perspectives on the SMC vis-à-vis the parish, community, and diocese.
2. Summarize the program's theology, and present a method for local application.
3. Offer a framework for committee spirituality.

B. Process

1. Small group meetings will yield action proposals.
2. Large group will scrutinize proposals in dialogic manner.
3. Components of committee will be chosen.

II. Preparation

As in previous sessions, the leaders must take responsibility to see that the room is arranged appropriately. If there is more than one parish participating, there will be a need for a separate room for small group activity.

Equipment needed for the sixth session:

• newsprint and easel

Materials needed:

• handouts for Session VI

Finally, as always, the leaders must carefully prepare their respective parts.

PROGRAM FOR SESSION VI

1. Prayer: 5 min.

This session's prayer focuses on the theme of discipleship and the Reign of God. This brief opening prayer intends only to center people in on the work of their committee as discipleship. It does so by repeating the scripture reading from Session I.

A. Introduction

The leader identifies the theme of discipleship and invites the group to hear and contemplate God's word as written in the Letter of James.

B. The Prayer Service

1. Reading: James 2:14–17
2. Question for silent reflection:
   How have I grown in my awareness of how to live my faith during these past six weeks?
3. Brief shared reflection.
4. Leader closes with spontaneous prayer.

2. Recap and Agenda Review: 5 min.

This is typically a cheerleading piece. The leader simply notes that this session concludes the program. It does so by leading the group through a meeting process, by summarizing several points, and by accenting the role of spirituality in the life of the group.

3. Components of Committee: 20 min.

In Session III the group was introduced to an organizational model for the committee. At this point in the organizing process it is necessary to solidify the group's structure.

The group must address two items: choosing (or reaffirming) the leaders, and deciding on the functions that the committee will assume. The problem selection in Session V served to set one key element of the committee's agenda, and the choosing of the functions that the committee will assume in the parish will fill out the agenda.

The Process

A. Introduce Task

The leader spells out the two steps that have to be taken, the selection of leaders and functions.

Choosing or reaffirming leaders is a sensitive task that the group should handle at its next regular meeting. Also, a term of office should be set with regular rotation established.

The second step—choosing the functions of the committee—will now take place.

B. Choosing Functions

Handout 6A contains a listing of possible functions which the group can consider as appropriate for their committee's work. There is also space for additional functions to be added according to the will of the committee. Be certain that the committee knows it is not obligated to include all of these functions into their work.

Review the handout with the committee. It may be that one or another function already is being handled by some other group in the parish. If so, this should be noted.

Systematically review each function, and test for willingness of the committee to include it as part of their work. For each that is accepted, identify a person who will be willing to be responsible for it.

Handout 6B provides a worksheet for listing the functions and persons responsible for carrying them out. As functions are selected, invite the group to write them on this handout.

Finally, add to *Handout 6B* the problems that the group chose in Session V.

4. Small Group Meetings: 45 min.

The small group meetings will give the committee a chance to begin to develop action plans to address the problems chosen in Session V. At the end of Session V the participants were asked to express their preference for their own involvement from among the priorities selected by the group. To prepare for Session VI they were asked to fill in the "grid" for the priority of their personal choice. In this session the small groups will be formed according to these preferences, and discussion will begin on what the small group will suggest be done to address the given problem.

The Process

A. Form Task Forces

The first step calls for the formation of task forces on each of the group's priorities. The leader simply focuses attention on the priorities chosen in the previous session, and invites committee members to choose the one they personally want to work on. The small groups or task forces then meet to begin formulating a plan.

B. Task Force Meetings: 30 min.

Each task force meets, and uses *Handout 6C* as the basis for devising an action plan. Each small group should be working to get a handle on the problem they are addressing, and to define the action steps they have to take in order to generate an effective response. The work they do in these thirty minutes is only the beginning of this process, but in this limited time, each group should be able to make a reasonable start.

C. Plenary Session: 15 min.

The entire committee reconvenes, and each task force presents its plan as it has been formulated thus far. At this point the leader will want to demonstrate how the task force and the whole committee can interact effectively.

The leader begins by asking for reports from the small groups. Subsequently, the others on the committee are invited to ask questions or offer comments on the proposals. In executing this step, the facilitator should be alert for examples of the committee members' possession of information helpful to the task force; for instances where committee members pose important, critical questions, or for other committee input and reaction that will help the task force develop a better plan. By pointing these out explicitly, the leader shows how the dialogic process can aid the committee.

This process of proposal formulation and modification can be promoted as a model for the committee to use on an ongoing basis. The leader will have to be aware that the amount of time allocated here for this is inadequate for the completion of the process, and will perhaps have to mollify some frustration that may consequently surface. Completion of the action plans becomes the next step for the committee upon finishing the training program, leaving the group with a very specific and concrete direction to pursue.

5. Break: 10 min.

6. Social Ministry Committee Perspectives: 10 min.

The Social Ministry Committee relates to a variety of other groups in the parish and in the community. This brief lecture highlights the SMC's interaction with several of the most obvious of these, and suggests ways in which the committee's initiatives can be served by establishing and maintaining these relationships.

Briefing Paper 6A contains the outline for this presentation, and *Handout 6D* provides reference for the group.

BRIEFING PAPER 6A: SOCIAL MINISTRY COMMITTEE PERSPECTIVES

In these few minutes, the leader should highlight the constituencies of the parish Social Ministry Committees, and the additional groups with whom they must effectively interact in order to carry out their mission. This lecture intends only to summarize these relationships.

Handout 6A contains a listing of these groups, and comments on each. The leader should introduce the topic by asking participants to refer to this handout.

I. Five Key Relationships

Read through each item with the group and embellish appropriately. The following notes on the respective items might be helpful in this.

A. Members of the Committee

The leader reiterates the importance of the maintenance function that the group's leadership must exercise. Accountability to one another will provide the backbone for the group's effectiveness, and to foster this each member will have to be affirmed, included and respected.

B. Parish Council and Parish Staff

The social mission embodied in this committee is not separate and distinct from the mission that the parish council and parish staff ought to promote. It should be one constitutive aspect of it, and as a consequence the Social Ministry Committee, parish council, and parish staff are intricately tied together. To foster this, each group should be represented among each other.

Councils and SMC's have often been at odds with one another. While some conflict may be inevitable, it can be mitigated, and the best interests of parish social ministry will certainly be served by amicable relations with the parish council.

Likewise, the relationships between SMCs and staff can be strained. As with councils, however, the establishment and maintenance of good working relationships should be a maintenance priority of the group.

C. Members of the Parish

The means used to approach the parish make a difference in how the SMC's agenda will be received. Sometimes the SMC will be tempted to browbeat the parish; at other times the committee will be so invested in a cause or project that the potential for disagreement will be keen. The facilitator should advise the groups to be careful in their approach, and realistic in their expectations.

Regarding the approach that is taken, groups should be reminded to recall that they aspire to fulfill their mission. The means chosen to attempt this will serve the group's purpose perhaps as much as the righteousness of the cause. One final point that parish groups often don't recognize is that every single positive response to an appeal is significant.

D. Community Organizations

From a sociological perspective, the evidence is very clear: church groups that influence society and work effectively on behalf of justice must work with other, non-ecclesial groups. One need not accept the *raison d'etre* of other groups in order to work together with them. In some cases there may be wide differences on concerns other than that one around which they are coalescing. Be that as it may, parish SMCs should be anxious to reach out and join forces with groups that share their objectives.

E. Diocesan Offices

Most dioceses have offices or agencies that deal with social ministry concerns. More and more they are seeking to work with parishes, both to provide resources and to build a diocesan constituency interested in working for justice.

Establishing reciprocal relationships should be the goal of parish social action organizations and the diocesan offices. The diocese has access to information and materials provided by innumerable national groups, including the United States Catholic Conference's Department of Social Development and World Peace and the Campaign for Human Development. Some diocesan offices provide ongoing assistance to parish committees, and can help the committee with its work in a variety of ways.

In many respects, the diocesan office also relies on parishes for its own effectiveness. Legislative networks, for example, rely on parishioners to influence elected officials. The parish can join in on projects too large to handle itself, and play a vital role in the success of important social change efforts by working with the diocesan offices.

A partnership between the parish and diocesan offices can be exciting and productive.

II. A Model of Operation

By referring again to *Handout 3E,* the facilitator can simply reiterate the concepts on the handout, specifically emphasizing the task force model, and the assumption of leadership responsibilities by various people.

7. *Theology Summary: 15 min.*

The leader here recapitulates the main points of the theology that has been considered in the program. Focusing on the process of theological reflection, and explaining how the process and content can apply to the ongoing life of the group are the two major purposes of this lecture.

Briefing Paper 6B provides the background for this summary.

BRIEFING PAPER 6B: THEOLOGY AND THE SMC—A SUMMARY

This lecture provides a perspective on how the church's teaching on public and social concerns can be applied to the work of parish Social Ministry Committees.

Already in the program, references have been made to the "See, Judge, Act" and "Pastoral Circle" models for church-based social action. These each provide a general framework for fitting the teaching into the process of social ministry. What follows can be considered to be an elaboration on the judging or theological reflection sections of these two models. It explores why and in what ways this theological reflection can be useful to the people involved in social action in the parish.

I. *Why? The Purpose for This Study*

A. Theological Grounding

For a parish-based social ministry group, grounding in the mission of the church is essential. Some measure of understanding of the theology of that mission provides one of the keys for a faithful response to the mission. Without this understanding, we lack the reference points we need to determine our group's agenda.

B. Church Involvement in Public Issues

The Catholic Church in the United States has in recent years assumed a new posture in relationship to society. Taking stands on issues such as abortion, U.S. role in Central America, nuclear disarmament, and economic justice, the church has joined in the public debate on areas where moral issues are at stake. As a result the church has been perceived accurately as being in some tension with our society. Consequently, this makes it ever more important for groups on the parish level to have a deeper knowledge and understanding of the church's mission so that they might interpret that mission for the parish.

This is especially true because of the role which lay people must assume in carrying out the mission. Vatican II's Decree on the Laity has made this point very clear, and John Paul II echoes the sentiment in *On Social Concern:* "It is appropriate to emphasize the preeminent role that belongs to the laity . . . It is their task to animate temporal realities with Christian commitment, by which they show that they are witnesses and agents of peace and justice."[1] For the lay person to do this, knowledge of the social teaching of the church is the necessary first step.

II. *How is Such a Study Useful?*

A. Group's Self-Understanding

With the foundational dealing with the theology that undergirds social ministry that this process provides, the group can more deeply understand the important and faithful implications of their concerns and actions.

B. Guidance

The theology can guide groups in deciding what they will do and how they will do it.

C. No Prescriptions

Neither scripture nor Catholic social teaching offers prescriptions for action.

[Draw the following diagram on the newsprint, putting the words up first, and drawing the funnel around them later. Listed are the sources that we use in theological reflection.]

---

1. John Paul II, *On Social Concern* (Washington, D.C.: United States Catholic Conference, 1988), p. 97.

Scripture	Inspiration
Vatican Documents	
USCC Positions	Principles
"This Land . . ."	
Local Bishops	
Parish	
Me-Us	Application

The various sources, it can be said, provide inspiration (scripture) and principles (social teaching), and some analysis (Vatican teachings, USCC). The specific application, however, gets worked out at the local level. No set program exists.

Scripture inspires us with a vision of what God intends for creation. It does not, however, provide specific answers to the complex issues of modern life. In *The Challenge of Peace* the American bishops capture the essence of the inspirational nature of scripture. They pointed out that the scriptures "contain no specific treatise on war and peace." Nonetheless, the bishops continue, "The sacred texts have much to say to us about the ways in which God calls us to live in union with and in fidelity to the divine will. They provide us with direction for our lives and hold out to us an object of hope, a final promise, which guides and directs our actions here and now."[2]

The principles articulated in Session IV provide fundamental measures for the justice of our society. Like the scriptures, however, the principles seldom find ready-made, indisputable application.

We inherit this tradition and scripture. It is part of what it means to be a Catholic. Yet, in the final analysis, it is up to me and us to decide how we shall apply it to our lives, and how we will activate it in our parish communities.

Further, we must take a faithful leap across the gulf that separates the facts from the faith. To apply the church's teaching with integrity requires our attention to the facts of the situations we address, and that compels us to be mindful of the ambiguities that will exist. Application of our social teaching is an imprecise art, making even

2. National Conference of Catholic Bishops, *The Challenge of Peace* (Washington, D.C.: United States Catholic Conference, 1983), p. 10.

more important our ongoing reflection on our experience.

To be faithful to our mission, we don't really have an option as to whether or not we respond. To be faithful we must simply bring our faith to bear on our lives and on the life of our world.

Convinced of our mission, yet aware of the imprecision involved, we can recognize the need for our decisions and actions to be rooted in prayer. (This comment provides the transition to the next section, *Briefing Paper 6C*.)

8. Spirituality and the SMC: 30 min.

Throughout the program, the group has used a variety of means and methods of prayer. This part of the final session intends to emphasize the importance of the spiritual dimension in the life of the group, and to present the approaches that a committee might use in its subsequent development. In addition, the underlying assumptions of a spirituality of social ministry will be explicated.

This spirituality integrates faith and action, the spiritual and the material in a manner rooted in biblical examples. *Briefing Paper 6C* provides the outline for the lecture and prayer service.

BRIEFING PAPER 6C: SPIRITUALITY AND THE SOCIAL MINISTRY COMMITTEE

This final section on spirituality should impress on the group the importance of prayer in the group. It is by no means intended to be the final word, but instead to present the significance of prayer in the life of such a parish committee, and to offer some methods of implementing it.

LECTURE

I. The Link with Theology

In transition from the section on the applicability of the social teaching to the life of the committee, it is noted that the theology is not prescriptive. Prayer can provide the bridge from theology to action. Through prayerful reflection, groups can gather the spiritual resources needed to carry out their mission.

II. Prayer-Action Dialectic

A. Prayer Must Be a Priority

Some may tend to equate active expression of social concern with prayer, or to suggest that action can take the place of prayer. At one time, the caricature of church social activists being all action and no prayer stood beside an equally stark depiction of charismatics being all prayer and no action. While these may have some validity in some cases, neither polarity can expect to sustain itself without the other. Social ministry committees need to pray if their actions are to be faith-filled ones.

B. Prayer: The Means to Conversion

Through prayer we come to discover God's plan for our world and for our individual lives. God constantly calls us to conversion, and prayer allows us to hear this call. When we respond to God, we inevitably act, and to respond faithfully to God revealed through Jesus Christ, we act for justice.

C. Prayer: A Way of Deepening our Commitment

John Paul II makes the point in his encyclical, *On Social Concern,* that for the Christian one's neighbor "becomes the living image of God the Father, redeemed by the blood of Jesus Christ, and placed under the permanent action of the Holy Spirit" (#40). Prayer leads us to realize this point of faith, helping us to see when we have found God in our neighbor, and when we have turned away from God in another.

Prayer deepens our experience, helps reveal its meaning, and nourishes us with faith. Thus, prayer leads us to a deeper commitment to God and to our neighbor.

III. Prayer Possibilities: Review of Handout 6F

Review *Handout 6F* carefully with the group. It provides concrete suggestions for ongoing inclusion of prayer in the life of the group.

IV. Prayer Service

Handout 6G outlines the prayer service that closes the process. The focus of it is the Reign of God.

The leader should introduce the prayer service by alerting people to the images which scripture provides us to envision the glorious Reign of God. Secondly, s/he can point out that it is precisely this vision which calls us to go beyond where we are. Sin intrudes in our world to prevent the full realization of this reign in our lives, yet the promise and the vision make us yearn for it. Finally, the leader can say that in our faith tradition, we understand God's reign to be both present and future. That is, we experience it now in fleeting ways, but await the final days to experience it in its fullness.

9. Evaluation: 10 min.

Participants will be asked to evaluate the program. *Handout 6H* provides the form for this. It is very important that this be done before the session ends. Generally speaking, few people would complete and return an evaluation form after the program ends. So spending time now on it is very important.

10. Closing: 10 min.

This provides the opportunity for the leaders to make any necessary final points. More importantly, however, it offers a chance for simply saying good-bye, good luck, and thanks.

Some groups use this time and time beyond the agenda for a party—wine and cheese, coffee and cookies, or some other variation.

Components of the Social Ministry Committee

A central role of a parish Social Ministry Committee is the identification of problems which the parish should address. This has been a focus of this organizing process. As the parish catalyst for the church's social mission, the committee also is the vehicle for other social ministry activities.

The committee should keep in mind that activating the parish is the central task. Accomplishing this doesn't require getting scores of people to join the committee. It probably will demand offering the parish a wide variety of ways to be involved. The following functions, if they are to be carried out in a parish, will most likely come under the aegis of this committee. They suggest just such a variety of involvements.

Possible Committee Functions

Education on Social Issues and Social Teaching: Raising awareness of social issues through educational means can be an important function. It certainly is an ongoing need in every parish. Also the church's tradition of social teaching continues to be something of a secret to many Catholics, even as it continues to expand. In 1988, for example, Pope John Paul II issued a new encyclical, *The Social Concern of the Church,* the Vatican issued a statement on homelessness, and the U.S. bishops have issued the first draft of a new pastoral letter. In 1989, the Vatican also released a statement on racism.

Emergency Assistance: Many parishes have existing vehicles for this function, but usually there will be some connection with the Social Ministry Committee. Other parishes may provide emergency assistance on an "as needed" basis with no organization at all. In any event, SMCs have to be attentive to this function, even if the responsibility for it does not fall to the committee.

Legislative Network: One easy way to get parishioners involved in working for social change is through letter-writing. Many diocesan social action offices operate networks which parishes can join by simply committing themselves to letter-writing efforts.

Social Concerns Fundraising: Each year a number of collections are taken up to support various social ministry efforts. In late November, the Campaign for Human Development collection funds self-help groups in the United States; and during Lent, Operation Rice Bowl raises money to support Catholic Relief Service projects in poor nations. Often these receive no special promotion. The SMC can, however, promote these efforts and increase parish support for them.

Respect Life Coordination: October has been designated as "Respect Life Month" by the U.S. bishops, and the SMC can serve as the coordinator of the parish's observance of it.

Other Possibilities: The SMC could also take on functions that help people relate the church's social mission to their daily lives in areas such as lifestyle, work and citizenship.

SESSION VI—HANDOUT 6B

_____ Parish

Social Ministry Committee

Subcommittees and Functions

Subcommittees   Functions

Problem Area: _____   Function: _____

_____   _____

Person Responsible: _____   Person Responsible: _____

_____   _____

Problem Area: _____   Function: _____

_____   _____

Person Responsible: _____   Person Responsible: _____

_____   _____

Problem Area: _____   Function: _____

_____   _____

Person Responsible: _____   Person Responsible: _____

_____   _____

Proposal for Social Ministry Committee Action

Members of Subcommittee: _____

_____

Problem Addressed: _____

Proposed Response (How the committee will respond to the problem):

_____

_____

Nature of Response (service, action, education): _____

Rationale for the Response (Why the approach was chosen): _____

_____

_____

_____

_____

Feasibility of Response (Why it is practical): _____

_____

_____

Resources needed to carry out the plan:

  A. Time needed: _____

  B. Committee members needed: _____

  C. Other people needed: _____

  D. Money needed: _____

  E. Other: _____

Action Steps

List specific actions needed to implement the proposal, including publicity, organizing, gathering of resources, further research, fundraising etc.

1. _____

2. _____

3. _____

4. _____

5. _____

6. _____

Social Ministry Committee Relationships

A parish Social Ministry Committee maintains relationships with a series of actors both inside and outside the parish. The level of effective interaction with the various individuals and groups will in some measure determine the success of the committee's efforts to fulfill its mission. The following explores the nature of some of these relationships, and points to ways that they can be nurtured effectively.

In each case the relationships are reciprocal. The accent here, however, is on what the SMC has to do to carry out its responsibility.

1. *The SMC and the Members of the Parish:* The Social Ministry Committee is not a group that will take on and carry out the parish's social mission. Rather the committee should serve as the catalyst that channels the energy and resources of the parish so as to fulfill that mission. The committee's role then is to foster involvement of parish members in social concerns, serving to educate and engage parishioners on a wide range of issues and needs. When people fail to become interested, the SMC should step back and consider how else people can be invited to be a part of the work.

2. *Parish Council and Staff:* Depending on the constitution of the parish council, the relationship with the SMC will vary. At times the SMC chair or a representative of the committee will sit on the council. At other times a council member will serve as a liaison with the committee. The structures may differ, but the key function remains; that is, the SMC and the council must maintain effective lines of communication in order for both groups to be effective in carrying out their mission.

   The parish staff also fits importantly into this equation. At times a staff member will participate fully in the committee's work, while at other times there may be little direct involvement. Without good communication and without at least tacit staff support for the SMC, however, the forwarding of the SMC agenda will be frustrated.

   Social ministry work cannot always assume the approbation of a parish council and staff, but to succeed, it usually will require gaining it. The SMC must consequently be sure to do its homework on issues it addresses, and it must pay attention to the links it has with the parish staff and council.

3. *Community Organizations:* SMCs are not competing with other community organizations. Many opportunities exist for fruitful, cooperative efforts. Neighborhood organizations often establish a base of support from within a parish, and local issues may be tackled successfully by building on such a base. Service organizations, meanwhile, can help SMC's provide services to needy people in a parish's area. A committee should be certain to know what organizations exist in a given area, and should learn about groups that are addressing problems that the SMC may have chosen as a priority.

4. *Members of the Committee:* The SMC as a body has responsibilities and accountabilities to its members. New members should be adequately oriented, and longstanding members should be sufficiently recognized. All members deserve to be adequately informed about important developments, and each person should be valued highly.

   Minutes are a useful tool to serve several of these purposes. They recall promises and commitments that various members make, and they provide an ongoing record of the committee's work.

5. *Diocesan Offices:* Various offices in diocesan structure have resources to assist parish social ministry groups. They also are likely to appeal to you for support.

SESSION VI—HANDOUT 6E

Theology Summary

I. Purpose of the Study
   A. Theological Grounding
   B. Church's Involvement in Public Issues
II. Usefulness of the Study
   A. Group's Self-Understanding
   B. Guide Group's Action
   C. Inspiration, Principles and Direction

Scripture

Papal Teaching

U.S. bishops'
statements

Local bishop

Parish

Me-Us

Inspiration

Principles

Application

SESSION VI—HANDOUT 6F

Spirituality and the Social Ministry Committee

The Role of Prayer

Prayer should be the foundation upon which a Social Ministry Committee's work is built. Neither a mere accoutrement to meetings, nor a formal addition to the agenda, prayer grounds the committee's work on the will of God. Jesus' prayer in the Garden when he said to God, "Let it be as you would have it, not as I" (Matthew 26:39), presents a model for our prayer as individuals and as a group. Even when it is most difficult to do so, prayer opens our hearts to God's will, and can guide us through hard decisions.

Varieties of Prayer

Prayer has many forms. From the quiet of contemplative prayer to the exuberance of charismatic prayer meetings, from the rosary to a folk mass, there are many paths we take to meet God in prayer. A committee should strive to utilize a variety of prayer forms so that the preferences of all may be respected and the spiritual lives of each member will be nurtured. Some possibilities include:

- eucharistic liturgies
- worship in word and song before meetings
- meditation on scripture
- centering prayer
- intercessory prayer
- rosary
- prayer services marking significant dates

Themes for Prayer

How we focus prayer can help animate our responses to social problems. Certain spiritual qualities tend to serve those in social ministry work especially well, and the nurturing of those qualities in prayer can help one both to endure the desert that sometimes faces us, and to celebrate the justice of God's reign. The following are a few themes that fit this category:

- compassion
- poverty of spirit
- God's option for the poor
- the goodness of creation
- God the Creator

- perseverance
- trust in God
- the reign of God
- Jesus' care for the poor
- discipleship

Times for Prayer

A Social Ministry Committee can make prayer a priority only by praying together. Planning to do so should be an objective of every committee: at each meeting, on days of reflection, special prayer services.

SESSION VI—HANDOUT 6G

Closing Prayer Service

Call to Prayer
    Focus: The Reign of God

Reading: Isaiah 2:2–4
    Reflection: How have I experienced the Reign of God in my life? Where do I see signs of God's reign in our troubled world?

Reading: Revelation 21:1–4
    Reflection: How does our group testify to the presence of the reign of God?

Song: "City of God," St. Louis Jesuits

SESSION VI—HANDOUT 6H

Social Ministry Committee Organizing Process

Evaluation

Parish _____

What did you find most helpful in this process? Least helpful?

_____

_____

Did you have ample opportunity to participate?

_____

_____

Could you suggest ways to make the process more effective?

_____

_____

In what areas do you think the committee may need further input and/or continued support?

_____

_____

Do you feel that this process has prepared your committee to do its work? If not, what else is needed?

_____

_____

For the following questions, 1 = strongly agree, 2 = agree, 3 = not sure, 4 = disagree, and 5 = strongly disagree.

1 2 3 4 5   1. This process met my expectations.

1 2 3 4 5   2. Presenters were well-prepared.

1 2 3 4 5   3. Process segments were purposeful and clear.

1 2 3 4 5   4. Handouts were useful.

1 2 3 4 5   5. The process has helped develop an effective vehicle for parish social ministry.

Do you know other parishes which might benefit from this process? If so, please list: _____

_____

After the Organizing Process

When the six-week process concludes, the parish social ministry organization is ready to stand on its own. The group will possess a deep understanding of its mission, and will have a more or less clear roadmap for the actions it will pursue. While a well-constituted organization will facilitate shared leadership, there is nonetheless a pivotal role which the chairperson and the parish staff liaison will play in the group's continued development. In addition, the group's periodic self-evaluation will allow for the diagnosis of impediments to its development, and will provide the impetus to make whatever change may be needed in the group's direction.

ROLE OF THE CHAIRPERSON

During the six sessions participants are encouraged to view leadership as shared among all members of the group. With the variety of task and maintenance roles which a successful group must manifest, it should be clear that no one person can embody all of them. Yet, there is a unique leadership role for the chairperson who assumes a set of responsibilities which are crucial to sustain the organization.

Selection of the chairperson should occur, if it hasn't already, at the first meeting following the process. The term of office should be specified, with one year and the opportunity to renew for a second year being a good guideline.

A good working relationship between the chairperson and the staff liaison will make a considerable difference in the organization's functioning. This relationship need not exist at the time the group selects the chair, but building it should be a major priority for both people.

The handouts from Session III contain key resources to assist the leaders. As presented there, the tasks of leadership include planning, administering, maintaining, and running meetings. The

chair and the staff person will together have to insure that these tasks are carried out.

Running meetings is one area where the chairperson will occupy the central role. Some of the specific tasks related to this role include:

- start and end on time;
- facilitate the meeting according to the pre-established agenda;
- enable all members to participate;
- stimulate discussion;
- facilitating decision making and insuring that everyone understands the decision once it is made;
- keeping the meeting on schedule;
- making sure that there is a minute-taker to keep track of all decisions and follow-up steps;
- seeing to it that tasks are shared among the members.

Other leadership tasks will be shared, more or less, with the staff liaison, and a key factor in determining the nature of this sharing will be the amount of time that the staff person allocates to the social ministry organization.

PARISH STAFF SUPPORT
FOR THE ORGANIZATION

Participation of a staff member in the process represents an important level of staff support. In order for the staff to follow up with this organization, going through this process is essential. A good measure of bonding occurs during the six weeks, and the common experience defines certain aspects of the organization. The staff person also brings certain resources to the group, as well as a specific role, which should be woven into the group's dynamic from the outset.

The parish staff person plays a key role in the follow-up to the organizing process. Short range, this will refer to planning and executing a commissioning service. We suggest that within two or three weeks of the process's conclusion that the organization members be commissioned by the pastor at a weekend liturgy. It can be very simple, and very brief. It does have the effect of giving public esteem to the members and the group, while also letting the parish know about the organization.

Long-range staff follow-up requires ongoing affiliation with the organization. Staff role will differ from members, and will vary according to how much time is available for the group. Enabling the organization members to carry out its mission is the essential function of staff, and the contours of that function will necessarily vary from parish to parish.

At a minimum, the staff will assist organization leadership in administration. Agenda setting, minutes dissemination, meeting arrangements, and reminding members of upcoming meetings are some of these administrative tasks which could be accomplished in three or four hours a week.

Other possible roles for staff include:

- nurturing the group's spiritual life;
- researching issues;
- providing a link to the full staff;
- facilitating ongoing group formation and education;
- accessing diocesan resources for the organization;
- aiding leadership development.

This list could continue, almost endlessly. To be sure, a full-time staff position could easily be taken up working with the social ministry organization. Since few parishes have allocated resources for this purpose, however, the general state of affairs in parishes finds a staff member with responsibility for this organization or area of mission as one of many. Making conscious choices about allocation of a limited amount of time, and making clear to all significant parties what those choices are will help a staff person be effective.

The staff person and the chairperson have the responsibility to come to an agreement on how the planning, administering and maintaining of the organization will occur. What that will look like

will vary from parish to parish, according to variables such as time availability and personality. The constant should be the explicit understanding between the leaders and throughout the organization on how these responsibilities will be handled.

EVALUATION

Evaluation is an essential function of any healthy organization. A parish social ministry group will benefit from periodic reflection on how it is doing. It offers the chance for both self-congratulation, and self-criticism. Most importantly, it lets the group consider what it can do to be more effective.

A new organization should establish a date three months from the conclusion of Moving Faith into Action for its first evaluation. In addition, it is helpful to schedule a one-year evaluation so that the expectation is clear to all that this will be a routine aspect of organizational life.

The group needs to be evaluating how effective its actions have been and how well its group process has worked. The following questions can guide such a review.

REVIEW OF GROUP PROCESS

Administration

—Are members notified of upcoming meetings?
—Are minutes of the group maintained?
—Are people aware of (and reminded of) the responsibilities they have assumed?
—Are meeting agendas set ahead of time?

Meetings

—Do meetings include sufficient time for prayer?
—Do they contain a self-education component?
—Do they begin and end on time?
—Are people satisfied with the space used for meetings?
—Do the meetings provide opportunity for open discussion on group priorities?

REVIEW OF THE GROUP'S ACTION

—Has the group spelled out its goals clearly?

—What progress has been made in this period toward achieving the goals?

—What means have been used to communicate the group's action to the parish? How effective has it been?

—Have others besides committee members become involved in projects of the group?

These questions can stimulate group reflection on its operation during the preceding months. As they are likely to raise many potential areas for change, the evaluation process should try to identify three or four areas which are most in need of attention.

Attention to the areas mentioned in this closing section will, we believe, provide a new organization with insight into several keys to carrying out its mission effectively.

Bibliography

Bausch, William. *The Christian Parish,* Mystic, Connecticut: Twenty-Third Publications, 1980.

Beal, George, Joe M. Bohlen, J. Neil Raudabaugh. *Leadership and Dynamic Group Action,* Ames, Iowa: Iowa University Press, 1962.

Bernardin, Joseph Cardinal. *The Consistent Life Ethic,* Kansas City: Sheed and Ward, 1988.

Brackley, Dean, S.J.. *People Power, Together We Can Change Things,* New York/Mahwah, N.J.: Paulist Press, 1989.

————. *Group Exercises with People Power,* New York/Mahwah, N.J.: Paulist Press, 1989.

Campaign for Human Development. *Daring to Seek Justice,* Washington, D.C.: United States Catholic Conference, 1986.

Catholic Charities. *The Social Teaching of John Paul II,* Washington, D.C.: Catholic Charities, USA, 1987.

Clifton, Robert L., and Alan Dahms. *Grassroots Administration,* Waveland Press, 1987.

Coleman, John. *An American Strategic Theology,* New York/Ramsey, N.J.: Paulist Press, 1982.

Coover, Virgina et al. *Resource Manual for a Living Revolution,* Philadelphia: New Society Publishers, 1977.

Donaghy, John. *Peacemaking and Faith,* New York/Ramsey, NJ: Paulist Press.

Dorr, Donal. *Option for the Poor,* Maryknoll, N.Y.: Orbis, 1983.

*Fagan, Harry. *Empowerment,* New York/Ramsey, N.J.: Paulist Press, 1979.

Finn, Virginia. *Pilgrim in the Parish,* New York/Ramsey, NJ: Paulist Press, 1986.

Geaney, Dennis J. *The Prophetic Parish,* Minneapolis: Winston Press, 1983.

Handwerker, Valentine N., and Julia A. Desiderio, *Every Day Compassion,* New York/Mahwah, NJ: Paulist Press, 1988.

*Haughey, John C. ed., *The Faith That Does Justice,* New York/Mahwah, N.J.: Paulist Press, 1977.

————. *The Holy Use of Money,* Garden City, NY: Doubleday, 1986.

Henriot, Peter, Edward P. DeBerri, and Michael J. Schultheis. *Catholic Social Teaching: Our Best Kept Secret,* Maryknoll, N.Y.: Orbis, 1987.

Hoehn, Richard A. *Up From Apathy,* Nashville: Abingdon Press: 1983.

*Holland, Joe, and Peter Henriot, S.J. *Social Analysis: Linking Faith and Justice,* Maryknoll, N.Y.: Orbis, 1984.

John Paul II. *On Human Labor,* Washington, D.C.: United States Catholic Conference, 1981.

————. *On Social Concern,* Washington, D.C.: United States Catholic Conference, 1987.

Kahn, Sy. *Organizing,* New York: McGraw-Hill, 1982.

Kavanaugh, John Francis. *Following Christ in a Consumer Society,* Maryknoll, NY: Orbis Books, 1982.

Keating, Charles J. *The Leadership Book,* New York/Ramsey, N.J.: Paulist Press, 1978.

King, Martin Luther, Jr. *Stride Toward Freedom,* New York: Harper and Row, 1958.

Meehan, Francis X. *A Contemporary Social Spirituality,* Maryknoll, NY: Orbis, 1982.

National Conference of Catholic Bishops. *The Challenge of Peace,* Washington, D.C.: United States Catholic Conference, 1983.

————. *Economic Justice for All,* Washington, D.C.: United States Catholic Conference, 1986.

Nolan, Albert. *Jesus Before Christianity,* Maryknoll, NY: Orbis, 1988.

O'Brien, David J., and Thomas Shannon, eds.. *Renewing the Earth,* Garden City, N.Y.: Image Books, 1977.

Peeler, Alexander. *Parish Social Ministry,* Washington, D.C.: Catholic Charities, USA, 1985.

Pemberton, Prentice L., and Daniel Rush Finn. *Toward a Christian Economic Ethic,* Minneapolis: Winston Press, 1985.

*Pfeiffer, J. William, and John E. Jones, eds., *A Handbook of Structured Experiences for Human Relations Training,* Vol. I, San Diego: University Associates, 1974.

Pierce, Gregory F. *Activism That Makes Sense,* New York/Mahwah, NJ: Paulist Press, 1984.

* These references have material especially germane to the content of the process described herein.

Sider, Ronald J. *Cry Justice: The Bible on Hunger and Poverty,* New York/Mahwah, NJ: Paulist Press, 1980.

Simon, Arthur. *Christian Faith and Public Policy: No Grounds for Divorce,* Grand Rapids: Eerdmans, 1987.

Spaeth, Robert L. *The Church and a Catholic's Conscience,* Minneapolis: Winston Press, 1985.

Tambasco, Anthony, ed. *Blessed are the Peacemakers,* New York/Ramsey, NJ: Paulist Press, 1989.

Weber, Herbert. *The Parish Help Book,* Notre Dame, IN: Ave Maria Press, 1983.

DATE DUE

HIGHSMITH   # 45220